Koireng Grammar

Koireng Grammar

Chungkham Yashawanta Singh

AKANSHA PUBLISHING HOUSE
NEW DELHI • GUWAHATI • VISAKHAPATNAM

AKANSHA PUBLISHING HOUSE
4649-B/21, Ansari Road
Darya Ganj, New Delhi - 110 002
Ph.: 23263193 / 9811582579 / 09435116718
Fax: 011-23263193
Email: ektabooks@yahoo.com
www.akanshapublishinghouse.com

Koireng Grammar

First Published 2010
ISBN 978-81-8370-239-3

PRINTED IN INDIA

Published by Akansha Publishing House, New Delhi and Printed
Harmain Offset Press

Contents

Preface

This book is a modest attempt to study one of the most endangered languages of the state of Manipur which has 33 various mother tongues. They are not yet fully or scientifically analysed.

The present study is the project of my second UGC Major Project entitled, Endangered Languages of Manipur: A study. The book is analysed in a descriptive model. It has twelve chapters. The first chapter is the introduction discussing about the people, the Koireng. The second chapter deals with phonemes of this language. The third chapter analyses about syllable and tone. The chapter IV deals with noun categories discussing about gender, number, case and different aspects of numerals. The chapter V deals with verb categories discussing concord particles, aspects, verb 'be' and auxiliary verb. The sixth chapter focuses on word class describing noun, verb, adjectives and adverbs. The seventh chapter concentrates on roots and affixes analyzing prefixes and suffixes; suffixes are more in number than that of prefixes; this is a phenomenon of Tibeto-Burman languages. The chapter VIII describes about word formation dealing with affixation and compounding in detail. The ninth chapter is sentence structures in which simple sentence, complex sentence compound sentence and conjunction are analysed. The chapter X analyses sentence process describing different types of functional sentences, namely declarative sentence, negation, imperative, interrogative, optative and exclamatory sentence. The chapter XI deals with reduplication. The last chapter talks about social grammar. In this chapter forms of address, naming system and taboo are described. The book has vocabulary list in two forms -Koireng to English as well as English to Koireng.

Author

Acknowledgements

It is a great pleasure for me to study the endangered language and it is also my desire to study such language. This will be a documentation. The wave of extinction of a language leads to the loss of a culture including its worldly knowledge and knowledge of the surroundings.

For this study I sincerely thank University Grant Commission (UGC) for giving me the Major Project to study the Endangered Language of Manipur. I am expressing my gratitude to Dr. H. Brojen for his ability as a project fellow of this project.

At last I thank my parent University and I sincerely dedicated this book to the University of Manipur.

Ch. Yashawanta Singh

Abbreviation

ABL	–	Ablative
ACC	–	Accusative
ADV	–	Adverb
ASSO	–	Associative
BE	–	Verb ‘be’
CAUS	–	Causative
COMD	–	Command marker
COMP	–	Comparative marker
COP	–	Copula
DET	–	Determiner
FP	–	Formative particle
GEN	–	Genitive marker
HON	–	Honorific marker
INS	–	Instrumental marker
LOC	–	Locative marker
NCP	–	Negative concord particle
NEG	–	Negative marker
NEGUN	–	Negative unrealized marker

AGNT	–	marker
PART	–	Particle
PERF	–	Perfective marker
PROG	–	Progressive marker
QUES	–	Question marker
SUP	–	Superlative marker
UNRE	–	Unrealized aspect marker
WIMP	–	Wish Imperative
1pp	–	First person pronominal marker
2pp	–	Second person pronominal marker
3pp	–	Third person pronominal marker

1

Introduction

The Koirengs are one of the earliest inhabitant hill tribes of Manipur (Gangmumei 1987). They are also known as Koren. They belong to the Kuki-Chin groups of Tibeto-Burman sub-family (Grierson, 1904). At present the Koirengs are found mostly in eleven villages in Saikul and Kangpokpi sub-division of Sadar Hills; the villages are Utonglok, Sadu Koireng, Nurathel, Iril Mapal, Ekpan, Tarung, Kamu Koireng, Longa Koireng, Awang Longa Koireng in Senapati Districts; Tarung in Thangmeiband and Lamphel, in Imphjal West district.

There are also some migratory villages namely, Longkuon at Langol hill which was shifted from Chingpei hill which is also known as Chetpan (living in active and prosperous). The name is believed to be conferred by the then Maharaja Chandrakriti. The Koirengs pronounced Chetpan as Ekwan and later the Meiteis called as Ekpan, Koireng at Nongmaijing hills. According to the 2001 census the Koireng population is 1487.

The original homeland of the Koirengs was known as Koram, the eastern land which is believed by some Koirengs to be the Koren state of eastern Burma (Gangmumei, 1987). The term Kolreng literally means 'men' or 'people of the east'. The so called Koireng has many alternate names as well as written in many forms, such as Kwoireng, Koireng, Kolren, Koren Quireng, Kolhreng. With the difference in spelling the linguists placed in different subgrounds. That is, Kwoireng and Quoireng are placed under Naga-Kuki subgroup of Naga group by Grierson-Konow (1904), under Western Branch of Kukish section of Burmic division by Shafer (1955, 1966), under Western Kuki subgroup of Transition to Naga of Kuki-Naga (Kukish) by Benedict. The Koireng spelling form of Kolhreng (Kolren) is placed under old Kuki by Grcerson-Konow and Shatfer, but Benedict is silent. Bradley (1994) placed Kwoireng in Zeiliangrong group of Southern Naga' group; he made similar to Liangmei (former exonym Kwoireng). He treated differently, that the other spelling form Kolhreng is subsclassified as old Kuki. Like Bradley, Burling (2003) also treated similar to Kwoireng so placed it in Ze group. As I understand Koireng, though having different spelling forms, it (Koireng) belongs to old Kuki. Because it has many points of similarities with other languages of its own subgroup.

The Koireng are one of the smallest tribes of India's Northeastern region which is a meeting group of various racial and cultural elements in this part of Asia. The Koirengs are referred by both the Chronicles of Manipur and the British writers. As referred in the chronicles of Manipur, especially in the royal chronicles of Moirang describe that the Koireng were powerful tribe in the ancient period. They frequently fought between the rullers of the Moirang principality. The history of Moirang referred to that they had several fights between the Koirengs and the Moirang king who were defeated by the Koirengs many times. Among the British writers during colonial rule, T.C. Hudson (1911) referred the Korengs as Quowing, whereas John Shakespear (1913) called them Kolhen. G.A. Grierson referred to them as Korrengs or Kolrengs. Grierson's Kolreng is very close to the tribe called themselves Koren. The Thadou called the Korrengs as Kolhen; the Kom called them as Karen. As noted the Koirengs themselves called as Koren and by this name they are known by their neighbour tribes like, Aimols, Chiru, Kharam and Purum.

Social Movements

The Koireng society has originally eight clans j(phung) namely,

Shong, Yei, Tieltu, Thamthu, Virei, Khonglung, Mreiem and Mikan. The village chief or the Khullakpa are selected from amongst the Shong clans and the Luklakpa forms an important village functionary amongst the Yei clans.

The Koren Chingsang Committee was establinghed about fifty years ago and the function was to preserve the costumes and tradition of the Koireng. In 1964 Koren Youth Organisation (KYO) was formed and the function was to train and develop sports and other cultural activities.

2
Phonemes

2.1 Phonemes

Koireng has 33 phonemes. They may be divided into segmental phonemes and suprasegmental phonemes. Segmental phonemes are six vowels and twenty five consonants. Suprasegmental phonemes are tones, that is, level tone and falling tone. They are discussed in the following relevant section.

2.1.1 Vowel

The six vowel phonemes are divided into three according to the height of the tongue as high, mid and low. They are shown in the table 1.

	Front		Central		Back	
	Rounded	*Un-rounded*	*Rounded*	*Un-rounded*	*Rounded*	*Un-rounded*
High		i			u	
Mid		e		ə	o	
Low				a		

Chart of vowel phonemes, Table 1.

Articulatory descriptions of these six vowels are given below:

i	-	High, front, unrounded vowel
e	-	Mid, front, unrounded vowel
ə	-	Mid, central, unrounded vowel
a	-	Low, central, unrounded vowel
u	-	High, back, rounded vowel
o	-	Mid, back, rounded vowel

These six vowels can be established on the basis of the following minimal pairs.

i/e	:	t^hi	'blood'
		t^he	'sweep'
ə/a	:	əy	'grind'
		ay	'crab'
o/u	:	noy	'crore'
		nuy	'laugh'

Some other minimal pairs are given below:

a/o	:	k^hay	'grasshopper'
		k^hoy	'bee'
o/u	:	kernom-nə	'agree'
		num	'also'
e/o	:	ke	'leg'
		ko	'nine'
i/ə	:	in	'house'
		ən	'curry'
a/u	:	ay	'crab'
		uy	'dog'

e/ə	:	kel	‘goat’
		kitən	‘save’
e/u	:	be	‘bean’
		bu	‘rice’
e/a	:	ke	‘leg’
		ka	‘room’
ə/a	:	məy	‘fire’
		may	‘face’
i/u	:	mi̤ci	‘salt’
		mi-cu	‘sugarcane’

2.1.1.1 Distribution of vowels

All the six vowels can occur initially, medially and finally.

Occurrence of /i/

Initial	:	in	‘house’
		inkil	‘fire place’
		inrik	‘wall lizard’
		incuŋ	‘roof’
		insa	‘cattle’
Medial	:	lim	‘sesamum’
		cil	‘saliva’
		rik	‘louse’
		ciŋ(muol)	‘hill’
		t^hiŋ	‘tree’
Final	:	ni	‘sun’
		t^hi	‘blood’

		arpi	'hen'
		saypi	'elephant'
		kirki	'parrot'

Occurrence of /e/

Initial	:	ek	'dung'
		el	'thigh'
		eṛtʰa	'October'
		eksan	'piles'
Medial	:	bel	'jar'
		peṛ	'kick'
		reŋ	'king'
		diel	'mud'
		ven	'today'
		pʰeṛ	'mat'
Final	:	be	'bean'
		me	'meat'
		ke	'leg'
		əde	'bright'
		uyte	'puppy'

Occurrence of /ə/

Initial	:	ən	'curry'
		əla	'stire'
		ətʰu	'rotten'
		əcəl	'male'
		əban	'next'

Mdial	:	pət	'thread'
		cəy	'spear'
		kəy	'I'
		nəŋ	'you'
		ṛəy	'axe'
Final	:	təkpə	'tub'
		puribə	'multiply'
		ərikkippə	'always'

Occurrence of /a/

Initial	:	ay	'crab'
		aṛ	chicken'
		aṛtok	'duck'
		aṛsi	'star'
Mdial	:	hay	'bake'
		lay	'naval'
		ban	'arm'
		naṛ	'nose'
		naŋ	'wire paya/ bamboo'
		wan	'sky'
		lam	'dance'
		yan	'night'
Final	:	wa	'bird'
		la	'song'
		ha	'teeth'
		kolsa	'lion'
		p^hurpa	'May'

Occurrence of /o/

Initial	:	o	'yes'
		olle	'or'
		oynu	'crane'
Medial	:	noy	'crore'
		col	'rest'
		boṛ	'some'
		zor	'kiss'
		wok	'beat'
		som	'ten'
Final	:	lillo	'joint'
		mitco	'blind'

Occurrence of /u/

Initial	:	uy	'dog'
		wuṛ	'snow'
		ucok	'frog'
		uyte	'puppy'
		wutp^hu	'dust'
Medial	:	ruy	'rope'
		zun	'urine'
		kum	'year'
		tuy	'water'
		wut	'ash'
Final	:	bu	'rice'
		yu	'liquor'

		lu	'head'
		mizu	'rat'
		wasu	'pigeon'

2.1.1.2 Vowel Sequence

In Koireng, vowel sequences are found in the disyllabic and polysyllabic words.

When the vowel **/i/** is the first member, the vowel **/e/** and **/a/** can be the second member. The sequence of vowel **/i/** and **/a/** are rarely found.

Example:-

i-e	:	bi-et	'berry'
		ə-si-ek	'put'
		ki-ri-et	'eight'
		t^hi-empu	'local physician'
		cə-ri-et	'mushroom'
		coŋ-ci-em	'fun'
i-a	:	ləy-li-ay	'medicine'

When the vowel **/e/** is the first member, the vowel **/e/** and **/ə/** can be the second member. It is also rarely found.

Example:

e-e	:	se-ek	'cow dung'
e-ə	:	əre-əsek	'keep aside'

When the vowel **/ə/** is the first member, the vowels **/i,e,o,u/** can be the second member. The sequence of vowel **/ə/** and **/i,o,u/** are also rarely found. (**/ə/** to a verb is a third person pronominal marker (3pp) and **/ə/** to others are used as a formative particle). Examples:

-e	:	ə-em	'green'

		ə-eŋ	'yellow'
		ə-ep	'squeeze'
		ə-en	'look'
		ə-en-nol	'revise'
-i	:	ə-in	'drink'
-o	:	ə-oŋ	'sit'
-u	:	ə-ur-olpa	'stepbrother'
		ə-u-rolnu	'stepsister'

When the vowel is the first member, the vowel /i/ is the second member. It is rarely found in Koireng. Example:

a-i : nai 'thatch'

When the vowel /u/ is the first member, the vowel /o/ can be the second member.

Example:

u-o	:	cu-on	'wo/a/rk'
		əru-ok	'empty'
		cəbu-o	'tealeaf'
		rəysu-op	'event'
		əloksu-op	'vomiting'
		bu-ən	'meal'

	i	e	ə	a	o	u
i		+		+		
e		+	+			
ə	+	+			+	+
a	+					
o						
u			+		+	

Table 2. Vowel sequence chart.

2.1.2 Consonant

Koireng has twenty five consonant phonemes. These consonants can represent on the point or place of articulation and the manner of articulation which are setout in horizontally and in vertical respectively. The consonant phonemes make distinction between aspirated and unaspirated especially for stop. It has distinction between stop, fricatives, nasal, laterals, trills, flap, semivowels etc. The consonant phonemes primarily show in six positions, namely, labial, alveolar palatal, velar and glottal (see table 2). It can be divided into voiced and voiceless. Out of these 25 consonant phonemes, the consonant phonemes **g, g^h, b^h, d^h, j^h** are borrowed phonemes. So they are found only in loan words. Example:

These 25 consonant can be established on the basis of the following minimal pairs or overlapping words. The following examples denote a contrast between the two consonants.

Examples:

b/k	:	be	'bean'
		ke	'feet'
		bel	'jar'
		kel	'goat'
d/k	:	'del	'mud'
		kel	'goat'
g/k	:	geju	'wheat'
		kedil	'heel'
t/b	:	ətun	'now'
		əbun	'pour'
		ətan	'run'
		əban	'find'

d/b	:	del	'mud'
		bel	'jar'
p/k	:	pəl	'gate'
		kəl	'save'
m/n	:	əma	'he'
		əna	'patient'
ŋ/k	:	ŋa	'fish'
		ka	'room'
		ŋəy	'sharp'
		kəy	'I'
ŋ/c	:	ŋəy	'sharp'
		cəy	'spear
ŋ/m	:	ŋəy	'sharp'
		məy	'fire'
		əŋəṛ	'hard'
		əməṛ	'fat'
p^h/t^h	:	p^həw	'shield'
		t^həw	'calculate'
k^h/t^h	:	k^heŋ	'plate'
		t^heŋ	'tub'
		k^həy	'bunch'
		t^həy	'cricket'
k^h/p^h	:	k^hur˥	'well'
		p^hur˥	'some'

c/l	:	ci	'hill'
		liŋ	'thorn'
		ca	'ten'
		la	'song'
l/ṛ	:	ləy	'tongue'
		ṛəy	'axe'
t/r	:	tuy	'water'
		ruy	'rope'
c/r	:	cil	'spit'
		ril	'inquire'
c/s	:	cəŋ	'right'
		səŋ	'blur'
z/b	:	zoŋ	'monkey'
		boŋ	'tree'
z/c	:	əzop	'suck'
		əcop	'wet'
s/h	:	əsaŋ	'tall'
		əhaŋ·	'fold'
g^h/t^h	:	g^hi	'ghee'
		t^hi	blood'
d^h/w	:	d^hon	'drum'
		won	'belly'
z^h/y	:	j^han	'cymbal'
		yan	'night'
y/w	:	yan	'night'

		wan	'sky'
y/l	:	yu	'liquor'
		lu	'head'
w/h	:	wa	'bird'
		ha	'teeth'
l/h	:	lay	'navel'
		hay	'bake'
m/b	:	me	'meat'
		be	'bean'
n/t^h	:	ni	'sun'
		t^hi	'blood'
k/b^h	:	kut	'hand'
		b^hut	'spirit'

2.1.2.1 Distribution of Consonants:

The distribution of consonant phonemes in Koireng can be analysed with the occurrence in initial, medial and final position of a word.

2.1.2.1.1 Initial Occurrence:

All the twenty-five consonant phonemes can occur in the initial position of words. They are shown in the following examples;

/p/	:	pət	'thatch'
		pon	'cloth'
		pəl	'gate'
		pil	'page'
		peṛ	'kick'
/b/	:	bel	'jar'

	Labial		*Alveolar*		*Palatal*		*Velar*		*Glottal*	
	Voiceless	*Voiced*	*Voiceless*	*Voiced*	*Voiceless*	*Voiced*	*Voiceless*	*Voiced*	*Voiceless*	*Voiced*
Stop Unaspirated	p	b	t	d	c	z	k	g		
Aspirated	ph	bh	th	dh		zh	kh	gh		
Fricative			s						h	
Nasal		m		n		ŋ				
Lateral				l						
Flap				r						
Approximant Semi-vowel		w				y				

		bak	'bat'
		ban	'arm'
		bal	'arum'
		baṛ	'some'
/t/	:	tiŋ	'cane'
		tuy	'water'
		tilpat	'leech'
		taytak	'west'
		toltaŋ	'couryard'
/d/	:	del	'mud'
		dəypa	'June'
		dayp^hət	'ulcer'
		dəyt^həŋ	'choice'
		duktoŋ	'fail'
/c/	:	cop	'lungs'
		cəl	'forehead'
		cəy	'spear'
		caŋ	'net'
		ciŋ	'hill'
/z/	:	zam	'black plum'
		zun	'urine'
		zoŋ	'monkey'
		zamp^hoŋ	'jackfruit'
/k/	:	kəy	'I'
		kel	'goat'

		kut	'hand'
		koŋ	'waist'
		koṛ	'ear'
/g/	:	gari	'vehicle'
		gehu	'wheat'
/pʰ/	:	pʰuŋ	'surname'
		pʰeṛ	'mat'
		pʰəw	'shild'
		pʰukləy	'breathe'
		pʰurpa	'May'
/bʰ/	:	bʰut	'spirit'
/tʰ/	:	tʰəŋ	'news'
		tʰay	'grasshopper'
		tʰeŋ	'tub'
		tʰəy	'fruit'
		tʰəl	'arrow'
/kʰ/	:	kʰoy	'bee'
		kʰuṛ	'well'
		kʰeŋ	'plate'
		kʰoppi	'town'
		kʰamul	'moustache'
/dʰ/	:	dʰon	'drum'
/jʰ/	:	jʰan	'cymbal'

/g^h/	:	g^hi	'ghee'
		g^həri	'watch'
/s/	:	saṛ	'dirt'
		sum	'mortar'
		sek	'farmer'
		səm	'hair'
		sok	'servant'
/h/	:	hay	'bake'
		hin	'here'
		hol	'sail'
		həycoy	'bring'
		hap^{h}oy	'grinder'
/m/	:	may	'face'
		məy	'fire'
		mitir	'mole'
		mirit	'tailor bird'
		muṛol	'club gourd'
/n/	:	nəŋ	'you'
		noy	'crore'
		nom	'agree'
		naṛ	'nose'
		naŋ	'sliced bamboo'
/ŋ/	:	ŋəy	'sharp'

		ŋakoy	'hook'
		ŋawok	'lata fish'
		ŋaprum	'eel fish'
		ŋaytoŋ	'cat'
/l/	:	lim	'sesamum'
		lok	'vertigo'
		lay	'navel'
		luŋ	'stone'
		liŋ	'thorn'
/ṛ/	:	ṛik	'louse'
		ṛul	'snake'
		ṛihu	'stream'
		ṛəmuy	'fox'
		ṛəmsel	'wild cow'
/w/	:	wan	'sky'
		wok	'pig'
		won	'belly'
		wut	'ash'
		wen	'today'
/y/	:	yan	'night'
		yəyni	'Monday'
		yamya	'fan'
		yamyəl	'tire'
		yiŋkeŋ	'morning'

2.1.2.1.2 Medial Occurrence

Out of 25 consonant phonemes, only 21 consonant phonemes can occur in the intervocalic position.

Examples;

/p/	:	kopi	'cabbage'
		kipu	'brother-in-law'
		əpol	'sky blue'
		əpak	'flat'
		əpəŋ	'solid'
/b/	:	əban	'next'
		əbəŋ	'white'
		əbut	'boil'
		əbom	'bunch'
		əbeŋ	'leak'
/t/	:	ətun	'now'
		ətan	'run'
		kitu	'spade'
		ətok	'touch'
		sete	'calf'
/d/	:	əde	'bright'
		ədəy	'like'
		əday	'cold'
		ədon	'bud'
		ṛoday	'dew'

/g/	:	lagaro	'go out'
/k/	:	əkuŋ	'stem'
		əkaŋ	'burn'
		əkəl	'climb'
		əkay	'incline'
		wakir	'return'
/p^h/	:	ip^hup	'spring'
		əp^hul	'boil'
		əp^hon	'bubble'
		rup^hel	'bow'
		t^həp^həl	'November'
/t^h/	:	ət^hiŋ	'swelling'
		ət^hək	'itching'
		ət^huṛ	'change'
		ət^hir	'die'
		mit^həy	'fly'
/k^h/	:	kek^hop	'shoe'
		ək^ha	'chin'
		ək^həm	'bank'
		ək^huṛ	'hole'
		ək^hik	'bind'
		mik^hoy	'break'
/c/	:	əcon	'duty'
		əcuŋ	'on'
		mici	'salt'

		micu	'sugarcane'
		kicoŋ	'jump'
/j/	:	əzoŋ	'fly'
		əzek	'line'
		əzop	'suck'
		əziŋ	'dark'
		moza	'shocks'
/s/	:	wasu	'pigeon'
		əsuŋ	'in'
		əsəy	'length'
		əsaŋ	'tall'
		əsin	'do'
/h/	:	əha	'fold'
		əhoy	'joy'
		əhan	'yawn'
		ərihu	'steam'
		ərihoy	'group'
/l/	:	əluk	'enter'
		əlak	'distance'
		əlum	'heat'
		əluŋ	'heart'
		selay	'gun'
/ṛ/	:	əṛiŋ	'neck'
		əṛok	'throat'
		əṛu	'seed'

		haṛuy	'gum'
		coŋṛil	'speak'
/w/	:	əwom	'black'
		əwoy	'flesh'
		əwun	'skin'
		əwat	'reduce'
		əwaṛ	'light'
/y/	:	əyək	'tame'
		əyor	'sale'
		əyak	'shame'
		beyaŋ	'soyabean'
		riyuŋ	'root'

2.1.2.1.3 Final Occurrence

Of the twenty five consonant phonemes, only eleven consonants can occur in final position of words. They are **p, t, k, m, n, ŋ, l, ṛ, r, w** and y.

Examples:-

/p/	:	jop	'kiss'
		rəp	'celling'
		cop	'lungs'
		koŋkep	'oyster'
		kelnəp	'dysentery'
/t/		mot	'banana'
		pət	'thatch'
		wut	'ash'

		mit	'eye'
		sət	'beauty'
/k/	:	wok	'pig'
		nuk	'back'
		sok	'sarvent'
		lok	'vertigo'
		sek	'harmer'
/m/	:	lim	'sesamum'
		sum	'cloud'
		lam	'dance'
		kum	'year'
		nom	'agree'
/n/	:	wan	'sky'
		wen	'today'
		zun	'urine'
		pon	'cloth'
		won	'belly'
/ŋ/	:	zoŋ	'monky'
		nəŋ	'you'
		luŋ	'heart'
		səŋ	'blur'
		naŋ	'slice bamboo'
/l/	:	kel	'goat'
		bel	'jar'
		del	'mud'

		pil	'page'
		col	'rest'
/ṛ/	:	saṛ	'dirt'
		cuṛ	'chase'
		peṛ	'kick'
		koṛ	'ear'
		neṛ	'mouth'
/w/	:	p^həw	'shield'
		t^həw	'calculate'
		əŋəw	'scold'
		mitcəw	'blind'
		ruk̤t^həw	'steal'
/y/	:	tuy	'water'
		lay	'naval'
		hay	'bake'
		ruy	'road'
		noy	'crore'

2.1.2.2 Consonant Sequence

It is the occurrence of two or more consonants beyond the syllable. A number of consonants can have immediate occurrence as given in the following examples;

/**p**/ can occur with **p, t, k, b, m, k^h** and **j.**

p + p	:	k^hoppi	'town'
		ərikkippə	'always'
p + t	:	həpta	'week'

p + k	:	nopkasik	‘future’
p + b	:	kip-bur̥	‘conch’
p + m	:	səmep-mi	‘barbar’
p + j	:	əliepjok	‘absent’
p + k^h	:	bopk^{h}ət	‘pair’

/t/ can have an immediate occurrence with **p, t, k, b, m, n, c, s, t^h, p^h, k^h, h, l, r** and **w**.

t + p	:	seratpi	‘cow’
		kutpi	‘thump’
t + t	:	inkotte	‘window’
		nitatteŋ	‘morning’
t + k	:	kutki	‘ring’
		nutker̥en	‘treatment’
t + b	:	mitbor̥	‘eyelash’
t + m	:	kutməl	‘finger’
		mitmul	‘eyebrow’
t + n	:	nikk^{h}ət-ni	‘day before yesterday’
		kumk^{h}ətna	‘next year’
t + c	:	kutcəl	‘index finger
		nitco	‘blind’
t + s	:	nut-sietwoy	‘disease’
t + t^h	:	mitt^{h}i	‘tear’
		sərietthet	‘pimple’
t + p^h	:	kutp^{h}a	‘palm’
		wutp^{h}ur̥əm	‘desent’

t + k^h	:	k^hitk^hay	'hang'
		k^hətk^hətta	'each'
t + l	:	kutlayta	'middle finger'
t + r	:	citrat	'fear'
t + w	:	nutsietwoy	'disease'

/**k**/ can occur with **p, t, k, b, c, p^h, t^h, s, l, n,** and **y**.

k + p	:	təkpə	'rub'
k + t	:	nəktip	'day after tomorrow'
		duktoŋ	'fail'
k + k	:	wokkicon	'hit'
		nukka	'after'
k + b	:	kəldakban	'step'
k + c	:	təkcer̥	'wart'
		nukcum	'delay'
k + p^h	:	mukp^{h}u	'inkpot'
k + t^h	:	rukt^{h}əw	'steal'
		əhoŋsikt^{h}a	'next month'
k + s	:	təksa	'body'
		yaksər̥	'bracelet'
k + l	:	lik-lisiŋ	'cork'
		caklenek	'food'
k + n	:	ker̥d t^{h}okna	'dress'
		hoŋsoknəmun	'source'
k + y	:	nəynakyokoy	'decade'

/m/ can occur with **p, t, k, b, p^h, t^h, k^h, c, s, h, l, r, w** and **y**.

m + p :	humpi	'tiger'
	ləmpi	'road'
m + t :	cemte	'knife'
m + k :	somko	'ninety'
m + b :	simbu	'owl'
	ətəmban	'score'
m + p^h :	simp^{h}oy	'middle'
	jamp^{h}oŋ	'jack fruit'
m + t^h :	kumt^{h}əṛ	'new year'
	somt^{h}um	'thirty'
m + k^h :	umk^{h}a	'bottle gourd'
	kumk^{h}ətna	'next year'
m + c :	nəmcənna	'quench'
m + s :	ṛəm-sel	'wild cow'
	somsəri	'seventy'
m + h :	həwarəmhən	'here'
m + l :	kumluy	'last year'
	ṛəmlon	'travel'
m + r :	somruk	'sixty'
	somriŋŋa	'fifty'
m + w :	ṛəmwok	'wild pig'
m + y :	cemyam	'dagger'
	səmyak	'molasses'
	yamyəl	'tire'

/**n**/ can make a consonant sequence with the phonemes as **p, t, k, d, c, p^h, t^h, k^h, m, n, l, r** and **s**.

n + p	:	benpum	'tur'
		wonpor	'indigestion'
n + t	:	sinteŋ	'north'
		inte	'cottage'
n + k	:	inkil	'fireplace'
		inkotte	'window'
n + d	:	nulcənday	'calm'
n + c	:	pənco	'brinjal'
		incuŋ	'roof'
		woncam	'appetite'
n + p^h	:	ənp^{h}uy	'a tree'
n + t^h	:	mint^{h}əŋ	'spread'
		kint^{h}um	'a tree'
n + k^h	:	ink^{h}aṛ	'door'
n + m	:	ənmani	'they'
		minmu	'show'
n + n	:	əwonnut	'colic pain'
		kinni	'two'
n + l	:	minli	'four'
		wonlien	'humble'
n + ṛ	:	inr˥ik	'wall lizard'
n + s	:	ponsil	'quilt'
		sinsət	'derive'

/ŋ/ can occur with **p, t, k, b, p^h, t^h, k^h, m, n, ŋ, c, s, h, l, ṛ,** and **w**.

ŋ + p	:	jiŋpi	'August'
		coŋpek	'order'
ŋ + t	:	meŋte	'cat'
		yiŋtieŋ	'tomorrow'
ŋ + k	:	məŋke	'tarmarind'
		laŋkiya	'eagle'
ŋ + b	:	coŋban	'word'
ŋ + p^h	:	pəŋp^har	'chicken pox'
		əhoŋp^hulyoṛ	'melt'
ŋ + t^h	:	luŋt^hək	'anger'
		coŋt^həŋ	'news'
ŋ + k^h	:	ceŋk^ha	'bitter gourd'
		əhoŋk^her	'increase'
ŋ + m	:	əŋmo	'what'
ŋ + n	:	soŋni	'Sunday'
		k^hoŋluŋni	'Friday'
ŋ + ŋ	:	kaŋŋa	'goose'
		riŋŋa	'five'
ŋ + c	:	t^hiŋcəŋ	'bṛanch'
		luŋciŋ	'knowledge'
ŋ + s	:	saŋsan	'mosquito'
		niŋsət	'glad'
ŋ + h	:	minməŋhot	'destroy'
		p^həywaraŋhiyəy	'breeze'

ŋ + l	:	kʰaŋlay	'cockroach'
		loŋləy	'busy'
ŋ + ṛ	:	coŋṛil	'speak'
		kʰeŋṛol	'stick'
ŋ + r	:	ṛoŋru	'back-bone'
ŋ + w	:	teŋwon	'cage'

/s/ can occur with **p** and **t**.

s + p	:	naspati	'pear'
s + t	:	wuysteŋdot	'dragonfly'

/l/ can have an immediate occurrence with **p, t, k, b, d, tʰ, kʰ, s, l, m, n** and **y.**

l + p	:	wulpi	'February'
		tilpat	'leech'
		ṛulpi	'python'
l + t	:	pasəlte	'boy'
		kultin	'nail'
l + k	:	kolkay	'sweet-potato'
		ṛilkel	'ask'
l + b	:	towulbuwol	'January'
		pʰəlbipʰa	'winter'
l + d	:	kəldak	'ladder'
		saldum	'mole'
		kəldakban	'step'
l + tʰ	:	rolthəṛ	'bachelor'
		philtʰət	'chair'

l + kʰ	:	yalkʰum	'bad'
l + s	:	kolsa	'lion'
		ṛilsuop	'express'
l + l	:	olle	'crocodile'
		lillo	'joints'
l + m	:	melma	'enemy'
		rulmintit	'centipede'
l + n	:	walolna	'January'
		kelnəp	'dysentery'
l + y	:	əhoŋpʰulyoṛ	'melt'

/r˥/ can occur with **p, t, k, d, c, j, pʰ, tʰ, kʰ, s, h, r, ṛ, m, n** and **ŋ**

r + p	:	kitəṛpu	'father in-law'
		kitərpi	'mother in-law'
ṛ + t	:	maṛtieŋ	'south'
ṛ + k	:	kiṛki	'parrot'
		wuṛkay	'bouquet'
ṛ + d	:	keṛdəŋ	'answer'
		keṛday	'play'
ṛ + c	:	məṛca	'pepper'
		kṛcat	'bug'
		keṛcu	'learn'
ṛ + j	:	keṛjor	'weld'
		tʰiṛjop	'magnet'
ṛ + pʰ	:	keṛ-pʰut	'decide'

ṛ + t^{h}	:	eṛt^{h}a	'October'	
		keṛt^{h}eŋ	'collide'	
ṛ + k^{h}	:	heṛk^{h}ət	'half'	
		kaṛk^{h}ət	'week'	
ṛ + s	:	koṛset	'deaf'	
		aṛsi	'star'	
		keṛsen	'divorce'	(d)
ṛ + h	:	keṛhuoŋ	'riddle'	
		t^{h}iṛhayho	'spoon'	
ṛ + l	:	ṛuolkeṛlop	'friend'	
ṛ + r	:	keṛret	'care'	
		əkeṛriŋ	'prepare'	
ṛ + m	:	keṛmu	'meet'	
		ədaṛmek^{h}e	'shoulder'	
ṛ + n	:	ətoṛna	'last'	
		keṛnok	'rock'	(e)
ṛ + ŋ	:	keṛŋoy	'red spinach'	
		keṛŋay	'thought'	
		keṛŋəw	'quarrel'	

/r/ can have an immediate occurrence with **p, t, ŋ** and **r**

r + p	:	arpi	'hen'
		p^{h}urpa	'May'
r + t	:	mertun	'April'
r + ŋ	:	waarŋoy	'heron'
r + r	:	əkarra	'between'

/**w**/ can occur with **b**, **k^h**, **n**, and **w**

w + b	:	k^həwbuṛ	'common cold'
w + k^h	:	t^həwk^hir	'again'
w + n	:	t^həwnarat	'courage'
w + w	:	seləwwe	'buffalo'

/**y**/ can occur with **p**, **t**, **k**, **b**, **d**, **p^h**, **t^h**, **k^h**, **m**, **n**, **ŋ**, **c**, **s**, **h**, **l**, **r**, **r**, **w** and **y**

y + p	:	naypəŋ	'children'
		ləypil	'earth'
		saypi	'elephant'
y + t	:	ŋaytoŋ	'cat'
		uyte	'puppy'
		tuytan	'current'
y + k	:	ṛəykol	'garden'
y + b	:	t^həybom	'grapes'
		tuybol	'bath'
y + d	:	tuyduŋ	'river'
y + p^h	:	dayp^hət	'ulcer'
y + t^h	:	t^həyt^hup	'apple'
		dəyt^həŋ	'choice'
y + k^h	:	ləyk^hət	'repeat'
		t^həyk^ha	'plum'
y + m	:	ləymay	'floor'
		ponsuymi	'tailor'
y + n	:	yəyni	'Monday'

		uyrəyni	'Thursday'
y + ŋ	:	ləyŋoy	'sand'
y + c	:	hycoy	'bring'
		cəyce	'tongs'
		t^həycaŋ	'a fruit'
y + s	:	rəysuop	'event'
		ləysa	'white ant'
y + h	:	t^həyhay	'mango'
		t^hiṛ hayho	'spoon'
y + l	:	ŋəyləy	'blunt'
		k^hoylieŋ	'wax'
		k^hoyli	'a big pimple'
y + ṛ	:	ləyoyṛəm	'desert'
y + r	:	ləyroŋ	'demand'
		moyroŋ	'marriage'
		sayraŋ	'Rhinoceros'
y + w	:	p^həywo	'air'
		tuywaduŋ	'river'
y + y	:	ət^həyya	'alone'
		ənoyya	'below'
		hoyyəyro	'wish'

In Koireng, three consonants can occur in the immediate position i.e. a consonant plus a consonant cluster. But it is found in a few words. They are given below:

m + pr	:	cəmpra	'lemon'

ŋ + kr	:	k^hoŋkraw	'trouser'
		kaŋtrum	'hokey ball'
y + st	:	wuysteŋdot	'dragonfly'

2.1.2.3 Consonant Cluster

It is the combination of two consonants within a syllable (intrasyllabic) or in other word, utterance of consonant sounds at a time. Consonant clusters is , like many other Tibeto-Burman languages, very rich in initial and medial position. But in Koireng, medial cluster is found in disyllabic, trisyllabic words and final cluster is not found. The cluster types are (i) Stop + Flap and (ii) Semivowel + Fricative.

1. Stop + Flap

It is found by combination of stops p, t, k, k^h + r

p + r	>	pr	cəmpra	'lemon'
t + r	>	tr	kaŋtrum	'hokey ball'
k + r	>	kr	kakru	'chalk'
			koŋkraw	'trouser'
k^h + r	>	k^hr	puk^{h}ri	'pond'

2. Semivowel + Fricative

It is found by combination of y + s

y + s	>	ys	wuysteŋdot	'dragonfly'

Koireng has no initial cluster. But final cluster is rarely found.

2.1.3 Complex vowels

Koireng has size diphthongs. When a semi-vowel occurs after the vowel **ə**, **a**, **o** and **u**, a diphthong like sound is created. Some examples are given below:

əw	:	p^həw	'shield'
		t^həw	'calculate'

		mitcəw	‘blind’
		əŋəw	‘scold’
		k^{h}eṛəw	‘quarrel’
		kicəw	‘bed sheet’
əy	:	kəy	‘I’
		t^{h}əy	‘fruit’
		ŋəy	‘sharp’
		cəy	‘spear’
		dəypa	‘June’
		ṛəy	‘axe’
		t^{h}əyk^{h}a	‘plum’
aw	:	k^{h}oŋkraw	‘trouser’
ay	:	t^{h}ay	‘cricket’
		lay	‘navel’
		may	‘pumpkin’
		hay	‘bake’
		way	‘chaff’
		saypi	‘elephant’
		ŋaytoŋ	‘cat’
oy	:	k^{h}oy	‘bee’
		əhoy	‘joy’
		coŋboy	‘dumb’
		oynu	‘crane’
		moyroy	‘marriage’

		ənoyya	'able'
uy	:	uy	'dog'
		tuy	'water'
		nuy	'laugh'
		artuy	'egg'
		tuyduŋ	'river'

3

Syllable and Tone

3.1 Syllable

A syllable is a vocalic unit or is a unit of pronunciation consisting of a vowel alone or of a vowel with one or more consonants. A syllable can be divided into three parts, that is, onset, peak and coda. Onset, it is the beginning of a syllable (it should be a consonant or semi-vowel). The sound **w** in **wa** 'birth' an **h** in **ha** 'teeth' are the onset. Like this the beginning consonanants of the following words like **pon** 'cloth', **ban** 'arm', **tuy** 'water', **del** 'mud etc. are the onset.

Peak is the nucleus of a syllable and it is carried by the vowel not by the consonant. The vowel, say **o** in **pon**, **a** in **ban**, **u** in **tuy**, **e** in **del** etc. are the peak (nucleus) of the very syllable.

Coda is the very sound which comes after the peak or the end of a syllable. The consonants, say **n** in **pon**, **y** in **tuy**, **l** in **del** etc. are the coda of the very syllable. In Koireng, only a peak can be a syllable or a word, for instance **o** 'yes' **u** 'a frog' etc.

Syllable segment

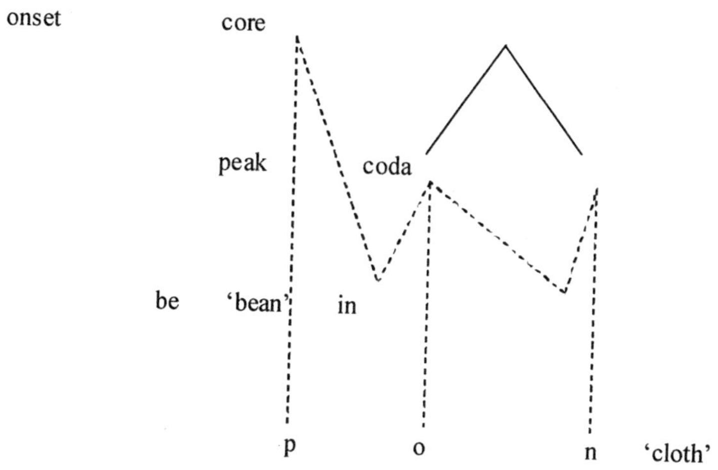

A syllable may be open syllable or close syllable. If the syllable ends with a vowel, it is called an open syllable, for instance, **be** 'bean' **ni** 'sun' **ke** 'feet' etc. If it ends with a consonant, it is a closed syllable, e.g. **kel** 'goat' **yan** 'night' **lay** 'naval' etc.

3.1.1 Syllabic pattern

On the basis of the vowel (v) and consonant (c) the structure of syllables can be divided into three patterns in Koireng. They are given below:

	Structure of Syllable			*Nucleus*
1.	v	o	'yes'	/o/
		u	'a frog'	/u/
2.	vc	ay	'crab'	/a/
		uy	'dog'	/u/
		ən	'curry'	/ə/

		in	'house'	/i/
		ek	'dung'	/e/
		el	'thigh'	/e/
		um	'tumbler'	/u/
3.	cv	wa	'bird'	/a/
		be	'bean'	/e/
		ro	'bamboo'	/o/
		yu	'liquor'	/y/
		me	'meat'	/e/
		la	'song'	/a/
		ni	'sun'	/i/
		ke	'feet'	/e/
		lu	'head'	/u/
		ko	'nine'	/o/
4.	cvc	pon	'cloth'	/o/
		bel	'jar'	/e/
		bak	'bat'	/a/
		ban	'arm'	/a/
		tuy	'tuy'	/u/
		del	'mud'	/e/
		kel	'goat'	/e/
		may	'face'	/a/

3.1.2 Syllabic Division

The syllabic division depends on preceding and the following environment of the syllable peak. Rules of syllabic division are given below:

1.	v-vc	ə-en	'look'
		ə-ep	'squeezes'
		ə-oŋ	'sit'
2.	v-cv	ə-la	'steer'
		ə-de	'bright'
		ə-nu	'mother'
		ə-t^hu	'rotten'
		ə-k^hu	'smoke'
3.	v-cvc	ə-ban	'next'
		u-cok	'toad'
		ə-yak	'shame'
		ə-wor	'throw'
4.	cv-v	ki-u	'elder'
		na-i	'thatch'
		k^hu-o	'village'
5.	cvc-cvc	zan-nin	'yesterday'
		kum-luy	'last year'
		mit-cəw	'blind'
		coŋ-boy	'dumb'

Regarding syllabification, Koireng has the following syllabification; monosyllabic, disyllabic and polysyllabic words. They are discussed below:

Monosyllabic words:

ro	'bamboo'
bu	'rice'

so	'key'
ke	'feet'
bak	'bat'
del	'mud'
pon	'cloth'

Disyllabic words:

wa-su	'dove'
kam-kəy	'leopard'
say-raŋ	'rhinoceros'
tuy-duŋ	'river'
sik-nir	'ant'
moy-roŋ	'marriage'

Polysyllabic words:

ki-no-te (trisyllabic)	'buffalo'
ə-hoŋ-sik-kum (tetrasyllabic)	'last month'
mi-rem-mi-kən-ni (pentasyllabic)	'Saturday'

3.2 Tone

Koireng has two tones –level tone and falling tone (level tone is not marked here and falling tone is marked as ‘). Koireng tone is found in some limited words.

These, two tones can be established by the minimal pairs as given below:

Level tone		*Falling tone*	
nuk	'back'	nùk	'pull'
caŋ	'paddy'	càŋ	'net'
moŋ	'a tree'	mòŋ	'hip'

cuṛ	'catch'	cùṛ	'noise'
in	'drink'	ìn	'sleep'
thi	'blood'	thì	'dead'
cay	'paddy'	cày	

4

Noun Categories

4.1 Gender

Gender is only a lexical feature in Koireng . There is no grammatical gender. It has no role in showing grammatical relationship between the nouns and other categories in the sentences.

Example :-

(a)	pasəl-te-ha	tuy	ə-in
	man-small-DET.	water	3pp-drink
	'The boy drinks water.'		
(b)	numəy-te-ha	tuy	ə-in
	woman-small-DET.	water	3pp-drink
	'The girl drinks water.'		

In the above examples, there is no role in showing grammatical relationship between the nouns and verbs. The verb **ə–in** 'drink' remains unchanged. It can occur with different opposite sexes i.e. **pasəlteha** 'The boy' and **numəyteha** 'The girl.'

For human being words indicate the opposite sex either male or female but do not posses any generic name. It is only a lexical item for example:

Male		*Female*	
kipa	'my mother'	kinu	'my mother'
kicapa	'my son'	kicanu	'my daughter'
əcapa	'his son'	əcanu	'his daughter'

There is a noun having generic names; male and female are indicated by the suffix **–pa** 'male' and **–nu** 'female' to the generic name.

Example :-

Generic name	*Male*	*Female*
sok	sokpa	soknu
'slave (M/F)'	'slave (M)'	'slave (F)'

In the case of animal, male and female are marked by suffixing markers; namely **–cəl** for male and **–pi** for female. But in the case of pig and tiger, the suffix **–təŋ** is used to indicate 'male pig' and 'male tiger'.

Examples :-

seratcəl	'bull'	seratpi	'cow'
ŋaytoŋcəl	'male cat'	ŋaytoŋpi	'female cat'
selocəl	'male buffalo'	selopi	'female buffalo'
saypicəl	male elephant'	saypipi	'female elephant'
woktəŋ	male pig'	wokpi	'female pig'
humpitəŋ	'male tiger'	humpipi	'tigress'

In the case of bird, male and female are indicated by suffixing markers; namely **–bar** for male and **–pi** for female. But in the case of **bat** and **owl**, the suffix **–təŋ** is indicated 'male bat' and 'male owl'. The suffix **–k^{h}oŋ** is used to indicate cock. They are given below: -

waakbar	'crow (M)'	waakpi	'crow (F)'
oynubar	'crane (M)'	oynupi	'crane (F)'
aṛtokbaṛ	'duck (M)'	aṛtokpi	'drake (F)'
tiktiniŋbar	'cuckoo (M)'	tiktiniŋpi	'cuckoo (F)'
kaŋŋabar	'goose (M)'	kaŋŋapi	'goose (F)'
laŋkiyabar	'eagle (M)'	laŋkiyapi	'eagle (F)'
kiṛkibar	'parrot (M)'	kiṛkipi	'parrot (F)'
simbutəŋ	'owl (M)'	simbupi	'owl (F)'
baktəŋ	'bat (M)'	bakpi	'bat (F)'
aṛkhoŋ	'cock'	aṛpi	'hen'

In the case of insect, the suffix **-cəl** is used to indicate male insect and suffix **–pi** is used to indicate female insect. But in the case of fly, the suffix **–bar** is used to indicate male fly. They are given below: -

rikcəl	'louse (M)'	rikpi	'louse (F)'
k^{h}aycəl	'locust (M)'	k^{h}aypi	'locust (F)'
pelecəl	'butterfly (M)'	peleppi	'butterfly (F)'
k^{h}alaycəl	'cockroach (M)'	k^{h}aylaypi	'cockroach (F)'
mit^{h}əybar	'fly (M)'	mit^{h}əypi	'fly (F)'

The suffixes **–cəl** and **–pi** are also used to indicate male and female of plants respectively as exemplified below: -

t^{h}əy t^{h}up cəl	'apple (M)'	t^{h}əyt^{h}uppi	'apple (F)'
t^{h}əy k^{h}ha cəl	'plum (M)'	t^{h}əyk^{h}api	'plum (F)'
t^{h}əy hay cəl	'mango (M)'	t^{h}əyhaypi	'mango (F)'
əwa t^{h}əpi cəl	'papaya (M)'	əwat^{h}əpipi	'papaya (F)'

4.2 Number

Koireng has no grammatical agreement in number. It has two numbers only i.e singular and plural. Singular is not marked overtly while plural marker **-ni** is used with the first person and second person pronouns to make a plural form. The morpheme **ən-** is prefixed to the third person personal pronoun to make a plural form with the plural marker **-ni**, as in the following:

Singular		*Plural*	
kəy	'I'	kəy̨ni	'we'
nəŋ	'you'	nəŋni	'you'(pl)
əma	'he'	ən̤ma̤ni	'they'

The suffix **-hay** can be added to the nouns or a word conveying the idea of plurality to make a plural as given below:

Singular		*Plural*	
mi	'man'	mi-hay	'men'
uy	'dog'	uy-hay	'dogs'
serat	'cow'	serat-hay	'cows'

The suffix **–təm** can be added to the nouns or a word conveying the idea of plurality. Consider the following examples: -

Singular		*Plural*	
ni	'man'	mi-təm	'many men'
uy	'dog'	uy-təm	'many dogs'
serat	'cow'	serat-təm	'many 'cows'

The suffix **–rikip** can also be added to the nouns or a word conveying the idea of plurality as exemplified below: -

Singular		*Plural*	
mi	'man'	mi-rikip	'all men'

serat	'cow'	serat-rikip	'all cows'
soŋkol	'cloth'	soŋkol-rikip	'all cloths'

There are some other words which can indicate collective e.g. **rup** 'herd' **buk/bom** 'heap', **k^{h}op** 'bundle' etc. example are given below: -

(a)	rup	'herd'
	serat-rupk^{h}ət	'a herd of cattle'
	wa-rup-k^{h}ət	'a flock of birds'
(b)	buk/bom	'heap'
	caŋ-buk-k^{h}ət	'a heap of paddy'
	rəy-bom-k^{h}ət	'a heap of flower'
(c)	k^{h}op	'bundle'
	micu-k^{h}op-k^{h}ət	'a bundle of sugar cane'
	t^{h}iŋ-k^{h}op-k^{h}ət	'a bundle of fire wood'

4.3 Case

Case is an important inflectional category of noun. It shows the syntactic correlation between the noun and the verb and between the two nouns in a syntactic unit (in the case of genitive). There are seven case suffixes. They are

1.	Agentive	-hin (pointed)
		-han (remote)
2.	Accusative	-hi
3.	Instrumental	-a ~ la ~ ŋa ~ ma ~ na etc.
4.	Genitive	-ta
5.	ablative	-taka
6.	Associative	-le
7.	Locative	-ə ~ lə ~ ŋə ~ mə ~ nə etc.

Agentive

The most widely accepted function of the nomination is to mark the subject of the sentence. Koireng has two types of nominative suffixes i.e. **–hin** and **-han**. The nomination suffix **-hin** is used to point out the action at present situation of the subject (to definitize) and the nominative suffix **–han**[1] is used when the action is remote (i.e. out of apparent) of the subject.

Example:

1. kəy-hin ŋa ki-cak

   I-AGNT fish Ipp-eat

   'I eat fish (present)'

2. tombə-han tʰahoy ə-wok

   tomba-AGNT. Thahoj 3pp-beat

   'Tomba beats Thahoi (remote)'

The pronoun changes their forms when the case suffixes are added:

Example:-

(a) kəy-han > ken

I-AGNT

(b) nəŋhin > nəŋŋiŋ

you-AGNT

(d) əma-han > əman

he – AGNT

(e) kəyni-hin > kəynin (inclusive) / əynin (exclusive)

we- AGNT

(f) nəŋni-hin > nəŋnin

you (pl.) – AGNT

(g) ənmani-hin > ənmannin

they – AGNT

Accusative suffix -hi

The accusative suffix is primarily used for denoting the direct object of a transitive verb.

Examples: -

3.	əman-han	kəy-hi	ə-wok
	he-AGNT	I-ACC	3pp.-beat
	'He beats me'		
4.	kəy-hi	əma-hi	ki-niəsiet
	I-AGNT	he-ACC	1pp.-love
	'I love him.'		

The accusative suffix **–hi** can be deleted. However, occurrence of the accusative marker is more commonly used.

Genitive suffix -ta

It shows the possessive relationship between substantives in which the preceding substantive acts as a qualifier of the succeeding one.

Examples: -

5.	kəy-ta	larik	khət	ki-wom
	I-GEN.	book	one	1pp.-live
	'I have a book'			
6.	hiwahi	tombə-ta	pon	.ə-ni
	it	Tomba-GEN	cloth	3pp.- be verb
	'It is Tomba's cloth'			

Instrumental suffix -a ~ la ~ ŋa ~ ma ~ na etc.

The instrumental suffix is used to mark the instrument while an activity is being carried out (by noun or pronoun). The suffix **-a** is occurred after the vowels and others are occurred after the consonants which are lengthened.

Examples: -

7.	kəy-hin	rul-hi	luŋ-ŋa	ki-thət
	I-AGNT	snake-ACC	stone-INS	1pp.-kill
	'I kill the snake with a stone.'			
8.	əma-hin	tombə-hi	nol-la	ə-wok
	he-AGNT	Tomb-ACC	stick-INS	3pp.-beat
	'He beats Tomba with a stick'			

Locative suffix -ə ~ lə ~ ŋə ~ mə ~ nə /yeŋ etc.

The locative suffix is to indicate the location of an object and event. The suffix **-yeŋ** occurs with human being while **-ə ~ lə ~ ŋə ~ mə ~ nə** etc. occurs elsewhere. The suffix **-ə ~ yə** occurs after the vowels and others after the consonants which are lengthened.

9.	kəy	iskul-lə	ce-ki-tek
	I	school-LOC	go-1pp.-UNRE
	'I will go to school.'		
10.	kolom-ha	tebəl-lə	ə-wom
	pen-DET	table-LOC	3pp.-live
	'The pen is on the table'		
11.	cawbə-yeŋ	larik-ha	pe-ro
	Chaoba-LOC	book-DET	give-COMD
	'Give the book to Chaoba.'		

The suffix can be added to the time also besides the space, as in the following examples.

12. əy-ni pun ko-ə ce-roy

I-PL hourten-LOC go-let

'Let's go at 10 O'clock'

13. əy-ni skul-lə puŋ riŋŋa-ə kərmu-roy

I-PL school-LOC hour five-LOC meet-let

'Let's meet at five O'clock in the school'

Associative suffix -le

The marker **–le** is used as a associative suffix which the action has been performed in conjunction with another person.

Examples: -

14. yayma tombə-le wa-ən-te

Yaima Tomba-ASSO come-3pp.-UNRE

Yaima will come with Tomba.'

15. kəy tombə-le ceŋ-ki-te

I tomba-ASSO go-1pp.-UNRE

'I will go with Tomba'

16. əma-hin bu-le-ŋa ə-cak

he-AGNT rice-ASSO-fish 3pp.-eat

'He eats rice with fish'

Ablative suffix -taka

The ablative suffix -**taka** is used in the spatial starting point of a direction or motion, source, expulsion etc.

Examples

17. əma bombe-taka ə-yo

he Bomby-ABL 3pp.-come

'He comes from Bombay.'

18. əyni-hin serat-taka serinutuy ni-som

    we-AGNT cow-ABL milk 1pp.-milking

    'We milk from the cow'

19. kəy-hin tuydaŋ-taka ŋa ki-cur

    I-AGNT river-ABL fish 3pp.-catch

    'I catch fish from the river.'

4.4 Numerals

In Koireng, numerals can be classified into two categories, viz. (a) cardinal number and (b) Ordinal number. Cardinal numbers have more complex and more formal structure where as the ordinal numbers are very simple in the formation of their structures. They are discussed below: -

4.4.1 Cardinal numbers

Cardinal numbers are used in counting, showing how many objects are specified as one, two, three, etc. It has two types: -

(I) Basic numeral and

(II) Compound numerals

4.4.1.1 Basic numerals

There are fifteen basic numerals. They are giver below -

kin-k^hət	'one'
kin-ni	'two'
kin-t^hum	'three'
kin-li	'four'
riŋ-ŋa	'five'
ku-ruk	'six'
sə-ri	'seven'

ki-fiet	'eight'
ko	'nine'
som	'ten'
riya	'hundred'
lisiŋ	'thousand'
lak	'lakh'
noy	'crore'
bel	'million'

4.4.1.2 Compound Numerals

There are three types of compound numerals. They are (a) additive compound (b) multiplicative compound and (c) multiplicative-cum-additive compound.

4.4.1.2.1 Additive Compound Numerals

The numerals from eleven to nineteen are additive compound numerals. It has a special marker **ləy** to make additive compound numerals. In this additive compound numerals, the prefix **–kin** of **kin-k^{h}ət** 'one', **kin-ni** 'two' and **kin-t^{h}um** 'three'; the prefix **–ku** of **ku-ruk** 'six'; the prefix **–ki** of **ki-riet** 'eight' are dropped, as in the following: -

somləyk^{h}ət	'eleven'
somləyni	'twelve'
somləyt^{h}um	'thirteen'
somləyminli	'fourteen'
somləyriŋŋa	'fifteen'
somləyruk	'sixteen'
somləyriet	'eightyeen'
somləyko	'nineteen'

4.4.1.2.2 Multiplicative Compound Numerals

There are two types of multiplicative compound numerals. They are (I) lower multiplicative compound numerals, and (II) Higher multiplicative compound numerals.

The lower multiplicative compounds are 20, 30, 40, 50, 60, 70 and 90. They are formed by the use of decade term **som** 'ten' multiplied by the basic cardinal numerals. In this numerals, the prefix **kin-** of **kin-ni** 'two', **kin-t^{h}um** 'three' of basic numerals have been dropped, then the prefixes **ku-** and **ki-** of the basic numerals **ku-ruk** 'six' and **ki-riet** 'eight' are also dropped. But in the case of basic numerals **min-li** 'four', **ri-ŋŋa** 'five' and **sə-ri** 'seven'; the prefixes **min-riŋ**-and **sə-** are not dropped in Koireng, for instance: -

som-ni	'twenty'
som-t^{h}um	'thirty'
som-minli	'forty'
som-riŋŋa	'fifty'
som-ruk	'sixty'
som-səri	'seventy'
som-riet	'eight'
som-ko	'ninety'

4.4.1.2.3 Higher Multiplicative compound Numerals

There are five types of higher multiplicative compound numerals. They are: - century, thousand, lakh, crore and million respectively, the **riya** 'hundred', **lisiŋ** 'thousand, **lak** 'lac' **noy** 'crore' and **bel** 'million' are the roots of hundred, thousand, lakh, crore and million respectively. In the formation of these numerals, the basic numerals are suffixed to the **riya** 'hundred' i.e., the root of century, to the lisiŋ 'thousand i.e., the root of thousand, to the **lakh** 'lakh' i.e. the root lac, to the **noy** 'crore' i.e. the root of crore and to the **bel** 'million *i.e.* the root of million. Then, the first syllable **kin** of **kin-**

k^{h}ət 'one' **kin-ni** 'two', and **kin-t^{h}um** 'three; the first syllable of **ku** of **ku-ruk** 'six' and **ki** of **ki-riet** 'eight' of the basic numerals have been dropped. But in the case of basic numerals **nim-li** four **ri-ŋŋa** 'five' and **sə-ri** 'seven', the first syllables are not dropped, as in the following: -

(a)	riya-k^{h}ət	'one hundred'
	riya-ni	'two hundred'
	riya-t^{h}um	'three hundred'
	riya-minli	'four hundred'
	riya-riŋŋa	'five hundred'
	riya-ruk	'six hundred'
	riya-səri	'seven hundred'
	riya-riet	'eight hundred'
	riya-ko	'nine hundred'
(b)	lisiy-k^{h}ət	'one thousand'
	lisiŋ-ni	'two thousand'
	lisiŋ-t^{h}um	'three thousand
	lisiŋ-minli	'four thousand'
	lisiŋ-riŋŋa	'five thousand'
	lisiŋ-ruk	'six thousand'
	lisiŋ-səri	'seven thousand'
	lisiŋ-riet	'eight thousand'
	lisiŋ-ko	'nine thousand'
(c)	lak-k^{h}ət	'one lakh'
	lak-ni	'two lakh'
	lak-t^{h}um	'three lakh'

lak-minli	'four lakh'
lak-riŋŋa	'five lakh'
lak-ruk	'six lakh'
lak-səri	'seven lakh'
lak-riet	'eight lakh'
lak-ko	'nine lakh'
noy-k^hət	'one crore'
noy-ni	'two crore'
noy-t^hum	'three crore'
noy-ninli	'four crore'
noy-riŋŋa	'five crore'
noy-ruk	'six crore'
noy səri	'sevencrore,
noy-riet	'eight crore'
noy-ko	'nine crore'
bel-k^hət	'one million'
bel-ni	'two million'
bel-t^hum	'three million'
bel-minli	'four million;
bel-riŋŋa	'five million'
bel-ruk	'six million'
bel-səri	'seven million'
bel-riet	'eight million'
bel-ko	'nine million'

4.4.1.2.4 Multiplicative-cum-Additive Compound Numerals

The numerals from 21-29, 31-39, 41-49, 51-59, 61-69, 71-79, 81-89, etc. are all multiplicative-cum-additive compound numerals. The marker **–ləy** is used as a additive marker. In this case, the first syllable **kin** of **kin-k^{h}ət** 'one', **kin-ni** 'two', and **kin-t^{h}um** 'three'; the first syllable **ku** and **ki** of **ku-ruk** 'seven' and **ki-riet** 'seven' respectively have been dropped, as in the following: -

(a) 21-29	somniləyk^{h}ət	'twenty one'
	somniləyni	'twenty two'
	somniləyt^{h}um	'twenty three'
	somniləyminli	'twenty four', etc.
(b)from 31-39	somthuləyk^{h}ət	'thirty one'
	somtumləyni	'thirtytwo'
	somtumləyt^{h}um	'thirty three'
	somtumləyminli	'thirty four',etc.
(c) From41-49	somminliləyk^{h}ət	'forty one'
	somminliləyni	'forty two'
	somminliləyt^{h}um	'forty three'
	sommiknliləyminli	'forty four'
(d) From51-59	somriŋŋaləyk^{h}ət	'fifty one'
	somriŋŋaləyni	'fiftytwo'
	somriŋŋaləyt^{h}um	'fifty three'
	somriŋŋaləyminli	'fifty four'
(e) from61-69	somrukləyk^{h}ət	'sixty one'
	somrukləyni	'sixty two'
	somrukləyt^{h}um	'sixty three'

	somrukləyminli	'sixty four',etc.
(f) from 71-79	somsriləyk^{h}ət	'seventy one'
	somsriləyni	'seventy two'
	somsriləyt^{h}um	'seventy three'
	somsriləyminli	'seventy four'etc.
(g) from 81-89	somrietləyk^{h}ət	'eighty one'
	somrietləymi	'eighty two'
	somrietləyt^{h}um	'eighty three'
	somrietləymili	'eighty four',etc.
(h) from 91-99	somkoləyk^{h}ət	'ninety one'
	somkoləyni	'ninety two'
	somkioləyt^{h}um	'ninety three'
	somkoləyminli	'ninety four'

4.4.2 Multiplicative Numerals

Multiplicative numerals are derived from the cardinal numerals; it is used when a question arises ' how many times and how many folds.' The marker **wəy** is used as a prefix to make multiplicative numerals, for instance;

wəyk^{h}ət	'once/single time'
wəyni	'twice/double times'
wəyt^{h}um	'three times'
wəyminli	'four times'
wəyrəŋŋa	'five times', etc.

4.4.3 Aggregative Numerals

In Koireng, the suffix – **rela** is used as a marker of aggregative numerals. It expresses the meaning 'two together or both', three together or all the three, etc. as given below: -

kinnirela	'two together or both'
kint^{h}umrela	'all the three'
minlirela	'all the four'
somrela	'all the ten' etc.

4.4.4 Approximate numerals

The suffix **–tək** is used as a marker of the approximate numerals, as in the following examples: -

k^{h}ət-tək	'about one'
kinni-tək	'about two'
kint^{h}um-tək	'about three'
minli-tək	'about four'
som-tək	'about ten', etc.

The word **ənimək le** 'or' is also used as an approximate numerals (or), as given below: -

kinni	ənimək le	kint^{h}um	'two or three'
minli	ənimək le	riŋŋi	'four or five'
səri	ənimək le	kirriet	'seven or eight', etc.

4.4.5 Repetition / Distribution Numbers

It is a partial reduplication of the basic numerals **ko** 'nie', **som** ten, **riya** 'hundred' and **lisiŋ** 'thousand'. In this numeral, the syllables **t^{h}um** of **kin-t^{h}um** 'three', **ŋa** of **ri-ŋŋa** 'five' and **ruk** of **ku-ruk** 'six' become **t^{h}i**, **ŋi** and **ri** respectively for the formation of repetition/ distribution numerals

Example:-

k^{h}ətk^{h}ət	'one each'

kinnini	' two each'
kint^{h}it^{h}um	'three each'
minlili	'four each'
riŋiŋa	'five each'
kuriruk	'six each'
səriri	'seven each'
kiririet	'eight each'
koko	'nine each'
somsom	'ten each'

4.4.6 Fractional Numerals

The word **suokkə** is used to denote the fractional numerals. But in the case of half and quarter, it is not used to indicate the fractional numeral, it has a special word **əher˥** as exemplified below: -

əher˥	'half'
əher˥k^{h}ət əher˥	'quarter'
kunt^{h}um suokkə k^{h}ət	'one-third'
minli suokkə kinni	'two-third'
minli suokkə kint^{h}um	'three-fourth

4.4.7 Ordinal numbers

Ordinal number are derived from the cardinal number by adding the suffix –**sunna** to the cardinal number except the **əcumtək** 'first'

Example: -

kinni sunna	'second'
kint^{h}umsunna	'third'
minlisunna	'fourth'
riŋŋasunna	'fifth'

5

Verb Categories

5.1 Verb

Koireng verbs can be classified into three on basis of semantics, namely, (a) action verb (b) process verb and (c) stative verb. They are discussed below: -

Action verb:

in	'drink'
cak	'eat'
ce	'go'
tan	'run'
peṛ	'kick'
woṛ	'throw'

Their occurrence in the sentences are given below: -

1.	kəy	tuy	ki-in
	I	water	1pp-drink
	'I drink water'		

2.	nəŋ	iskul	ni-ce
	you	school	2pp.-go
	'You go to school'		
3.	əma	bu	ə-cak
	he	rice	3pp-eat
	'He eats rice'		

Process Verb

suoŋ	'cook'
sinsək	'prepare'
min	'ripe'
sen	'blow'

Their occurrence in the sentences: -

4.	t^həyhay-ha	ə-min	
	mango-DET	3pp.-ripe	
	'The mango is ripe'		
5.	kəy	bu	ki-suoŋ
	I	rice	Ipp-cook
	'I cook rice.'		

Stative Verb

day	'cold'
lien	'big'
sin	'small'
rik	'heavy'

Their occurrences in the sentences are given here: -

6.	t^hiŋha	ə-lien
	tree-DET	3pp-big
	'The tree is big'	
7.	soŋkol-hi	ə-sin
	shirt-DET	3pp-small
	'This shirt is small'	

5.2 Aspect

Aspect is more predominant in Koireng. In Tibeto-Burman languages, tense, in general, is not distinctive as it is in the languages like English, Hindi, Sanskrit etc. Consider the following examples: -

8.	kəy	wen	iskul	ki-ce
	I	today	school	1pp-go
	'I go to school today.'			
9.	kəy	yantieŋ	iskul	ki-ce
	I	yesterday	school	1pp-go
	'I went to school yesterday.'			

In the above two sentences, the verb **ki-ce** 'go' remains same though they occur with different adverbial time **wen** 'today' and **yantieŋ** 'yesterday' respectively.

There are some morphmes, that is, **-te** indicating progressive, **-yəy** indicating completed and **–te** indicating unrealized. However, smantic tense can be realizd. It is more convenient to describe aspect not tense in Koireng. In this language, there are four aspects. They are (i) Simple aspect, (ii) Progressive aspect, (iii) Perfective aspect and (iv) Unrealized or irrealis aspects. They are discussed below: -

I. Simple Aspect

It expresses simple statement, habitual meaning, universal truth and routine action. In Koireng, simple aspect is indicated by zero morpheme but pronominal prefix is a must, prefixed to the verb as exemplified below: -

10.	kəy	bu	ki-cak
	I	rice	1pp-eat
	'I eat rice.'		

11.	əma	tuy	ə-in
	He	water	3pp.-drink
	'He drinks water.'		

II. Progressive Aspect

This is indicated by –**lə**. It expresses the action is continuing. Consider the following examples: -

12.	kəy	ki-lə-ce
	I	Ipp-PROG.-go
	'I am going.'	

13.	nəŋ	bu	ni-le-suoŋ
	you	rice	2pp-PROG.-cook
	'You are cooking rice.'		

14.	əma	bu	ə-lə-suoŋ
	he	rice	3pp-PROG.-cook
	'He is cooking rice.'		

III. Perfective Aspect

It is expressed by the suffix –**yəy** which occurs after the main verb, for instance;

15.	kəy	cuom-hɑ	ki-tʰo-yəy
	I	work-DET	1pp-do-PERF.
	'I have finished the work.'		

16. əma ven ə-yoŋ-yəy
he today 3pp-come-PERF
'He has come today.'

IV. Unrealised or Irrealis Aspect

It is used for action which will take place in the near future. The relevant aspect marker is **–te** which is suffixed to the verb, not prefixed to the verb. This aspect markers is quite different from the other aspect markers. Example:-

17. kəy iskul cey-ki-te
I school go-1pp-UNRE.
'I will go to school.'

18. əma bu cak-ə-te
he rice eat-3pp-UNRE
'He will eat rice.'

5.3 Verb 'be'

In Koireng, the verb 'be' can function as copulative verb. It is a linking verb. It links the subject to a complement. The suffix **–ni** functions as a copulative verb, 'to indicate the proper noun, pronoun, identification, class membership, class inclusion, cardinal number, ordinal number, etc. They are given below:

A. Proper Noun

Examples:

19. rəm-ha imphal ə–ni
land-DET. Imphal 3pp-BE
'This land is Imphal.'

20. rəm-ha delhi ə–ni
land-DET. Delhi 3pp-BE
'That land is Delhi.'

B. Pronoun

Examples:

21.	pon-ha	kəyta	ə–ni
	cloth-DET.	my	3pp-BE
	'That cloth is mine.'		
22.	oŋ-ha	kəy	ki-ni
	sit-DET.	I	1pp-BE
	'I am the teacher (that teacher is me)'		

C. Identification

Examples:

23.	kəy	cawbə	ki-ni
	I	chaoba	1pp-BE
	'I am Chaoba'		
24.	əma	tombə	ə–ni
	he	tomba	3pp-BE
	'He is Tomba'		

D. Class membership

Examples:

25.	ənmani	ləwmi	ən-ni
	They	farmer	3pp-BE
	They are farmers.'		
26.	ənmani	niŋsək	ən-ni
	They	thief	3pp-BE
	'They are thieves.'		

27. dəktər-ha pasəl ə–ni
doctor-DET. man 3pp-BE
'That doctor is a man.'

28. dəktər-ha numəy ə–ni
doctor-DET woman 3pp-BE
'That doctor is a woman.'

E. Cardinal Number

Examples:

29. kəyni unay səri kin-ni
we sibling seven 2pp-BE
'We are seven sibling.'

30. ənmani mi minli ən-ni
They man four 3pp-BE
'They are four person.'

F. Ordinal

Examles:

31. pasəlte̤ha kint^{h}um-suna ə–ni
boy-DET. three-comp. 3pp-BE
'That boy is the third one.'

32. numəyte-ha minli-suna ə–ni
girl-DET. four-comp. 3pp.-BE
'That girl is the fourth one.'

From the above sentences it is learnt that even to the copula **–ni** the verbal pronominal marker is prefixed according to the personal pronoun (that is, **ki-** for the first person, **ni-** for the second person and **ə–** for the third person).

The copulative verb **–ni** can also occur in the interrogative sentences as exemplified below:

33.	hawaha	uy-mo	ə–ni
	that	dog-QUES	3pp-BE

'Is that a dog?'

34.	larik-ha	hiwahi-mo	ə–ni
	book-DET.	this-QUES.	3pp-BE

'Is this the book?'

5.4 Auxiliary Verb

In Koireng, there are two types of auxiliary verb. They are **əsa** 'may' and **tor** 'can'. They are discussed below:

I. əsa 'may' which does not need prominal marker in-the construction. Examples:

The auxiliary verb **əsa** 'may' occurs after the main verb.

Examples: -

35.	kəy	bu	cak	əsa
	I	rice	eat	may

'I may eat rice'

36.	əma	iskul	ce	əsa
	he	school	go	may

'He may go to school'

37.	kəy	wa	əsa
	I	come	may

'I may come'

II. -toṛ 'can'

The auxiliary verb **-tor** 'can' is suffixed to the verb. It, **-tor**, is different from **əsa** 'may' which is not a suffix nor a prefix. In the case of the anxiliary, **–tor,** 'can' pronominal marker is found necessary for the respective personal pronouns. Besides it, the sentene is kept in unrealized aspect which is suffixed to the pronominal maker, like **kit + te (1pp + UNRE), nə + te (2pp + UNRE)** and **ə + te (3pp + UNRE)** which ends the construction. Example: -

38. kəy wa-toṛ ki-te
    I come-can Ipp-UNRE.
    'I can came'

39. əma in-toṛ ə-te
    he drink-can 3pp-UNRE.
    'He can drink.'

40. nəŋ ce-toṛ ni-te
    you go-can 2pp-UNRE.
    'you can go'

Here it is seen that the auxiliary **–tor** 'can' is added to the verb and the respective pronomimal markers are occurred in the sentences, at the same time prominal markers occurs with the unrealized aspect.

6

Word Class

6.1 Noun

In Koireng, there are two classes of noun on the basis of their structural nature, namely, (a) Simple Nouns,(b) Derived Nouns and (c) Compound Nouns.

Simple nouns are the single free roots and cannot be further divided into a simpler form, for instance; **uy** 'dog', **pon** 'cloth' **ni** 'sun' etc.

Derived nouns are formed by affixation.

Affixation

(a)	cak	'eat'	ə-cak	'eater'
	in	'drink'	ə-in	'drinker'
	i	'write'	ə-I	'writer'
	pa	'read'	ə-pa	'reader'
	ce	'go'	ə-ce	'walker'
	tan	'rum'	ə-tan	'runner'
	kap	'shoot'	ə-kap'	'shooter'
	ril	'speak'	ə-ril	'speaker'

(ə- indicates 'actor' or 'agent')

(b)	ril	'speak'	əni-ril	'manner of speaking'
	cak	'eat'	əni-cak	'manner of eating'
	pa	'read'	əni-pa	'manner of reading'
	in	'drink'	əni-in	'manner of drinking'
	ce	'go walk'	əni-ce	'manner of digging'
	əcay	'dig'	əni-əcay	'manner of digging'
	ətan	'cut'	əni-ətan	'manner of cutting'

(**əni-** indicates the manner or mode of action).

Compounding

(a) Noun + Noun

serat + me	>	seratme	'beef'
cow flesh			
mit + mul	>	mitmul	'eyelash'
eye body hair			
in + sa	>	insa	'domestic animal'
house animal			
ar + tuy	>	artuy	'egg'
hen water			
t^hiŋ + kor	>	t^hiŋkor	'bark'
tree ear			

(b) Noun + Diminutive [te 'small']

uy + te	>	uyte	'puppy'
dog			
se + te	>	sete	'calf'
cow			

pəsəl + te > pəsəlte 'boy'

man

numəy + te > numəyte 'girl'

women

in + te > inte 'cottage'

house

tukal + te > tukal-te 'small shop'

shop

ya + te > ya-te 'small fish'

fish

(c) Adjective + Noun

rəm + wok > rəmwok 'wild' (boar)

rəm + ar˥tok > rəmartok 'wild duck'

(d) Noun + Adjettive

kum + əthər > kumthər 'new year

year new

kum + əban > kumban 'next year'

year next

(e) Noun + Verb

ar + cak > ar˥cak 'ring worm'

hen eat

in + sək > insək ' house maker'

house make

t^{h}iŋ + t^{h}o > t^{h}iŋt^{h}o 'carpenter'

tree work

pon +k^hoŋ	>	ponk^{h}oŋ	'weaver'
cloth weave			

(f) Noun + Augmentation

uy + lien	>	uylien	'big dog'
dog big			
in +lien	>	inline	'big house'
house big			
ŋa + lien	>	ŋalien	'big fish'
fish big			
tuy + lien	>	tuylien	'flood'
water big			
se +lien	>	selien	'big cow'
cow big			

6.2 Verb

Verbs in this language are not bound. All the aspect markers are suffixed to the berb while the pronominal markers are prefixed to i.e., (it is a pronominal language). It has three types (a) action verb (b) Process verb and (c) stative verb. (see for detal in Verb 5.1)

6.3 Adjectives

In Koireng, there are three forms of comparison in adjective. They are positive form, comparative form and superlative form. In positive form, there is no marker. However, the degree of comparison i.e. comparative and superlative are marked morphologically by adding the suffixes **–det**. and –**kodok** to the positive form respectively but Manipuri has no morphological marker for indicating comparative as well as superlative degree. Example:-

Positive		*Comparative*		*Superlative*	
sa	'good'	sa-det	'better'	sa-kodok	'best'
ciŋ	'wise'	ciŋ-det	'wiser'	ciŋ-kodok	'wisest'

ril	'red'	ril-det	'redder'	ril-kodok	'reddest'
lum	'hot'	lum-det	'hotter'	lum-kodok	'hottest'
boŋ	'short'	boŋ-det	'shorter'	boŋ-kodok	'shortest'
səy	'long'	səy-det	'longer'	səy-kodok	'longest'
em	'green'	em-det	'greener'	em-kodok	'greenest'
day	'cold'	day-det	'cooler'	day-kodok	'coolest'
saŋ	'tall'	saŋ-det	'taller'	saŋ-kodok	'tallest'
lien	'big'	lien-det	'bigger'	lien-kodok	'bigger'

The degree of comparison are showed in the sentence level: -

1. k^hahoy –sa

   khahoi 3pp-tall

   'Khahoi is tall.'

2. k^hahoy kəy-nekin ə–saŋ-det

   khahoi I-from 3pp-tall-COMP.

   'Khahoi is taller than me.'

3. k^hahoy kyni-nekin ə–saŋ-kodok

   khahoi we-from 3pp-tall-SUP.

   'Khahoi is the tallest among us.'

6.4 Adverbs

In Koireng, the suffixes **–təkkə/-yə~mə~nə** etc. mark as an adverb marker. The prefix **əneka**- and **ək^{h}ella**, the suffix **–detta/ -yə~mə~nə** etc. and **–detin /~yə~mə~nə** etc. are used for the comparison of adverbs as exemplified below:

sət-təkkə	əneka-sət-detta	ək^{h}ela-sət-detin
'nicely'	'more nicely'	'nost nicely'
rəp-təkkə	əneka-rəp-detta	ək^{h}ela-rəp-detin

'quickly'	'more quickly'	'most quickly'
yam-təkkə	əneka-yam-detta	ək^{h}ela-yam-detin
'slowly'	'more slowly'	'most slowly'
ciŋ-təkkə	əneka-ciŋ-detta	ək^{h}ela-ciŋ-detin
'wisely'	'more wisely'	'most wisely'

Examples:

4. əma rəp-təkkə ə–ce
   he quick-ADV. 3pp-go
   'He goes quickly.'

5. əma nekə-rəp-detta ə–ce
   he more-quick-ADV 3pp-go
   'He goes more quickly.'

6. əma ək^{h}ela-rəp-detin ə–ce
   he most –quick-ADV. 3pp-go
   'He goes very quickly.'

Adverb of time

ətun	'now'
wen	'today'
yan-nin	'yesterday'
ya-tieŋ	'tomorrow'
kumk^{h}ətna	'next year'
kumluy	'last year'

Adverb of Place

hiwahi	'here'
hawaha	'there'
hunəmo	'where' etc.

8

Roots and Affixes

7.1 Roots

Root: A root is a form which is not further analyzable either in terms of derivational or inflectional morphology. A root is the basic part always present in a lexeme. The root can be classified into two types i.e. free root and bound root.

In this language, the free root can be found in monosyllabic, disyllabic and polysyllabic words.

Free root

a. Monosyllabic free root

uy	'dog'
wa	'bird'
be	'bean'
ke	'feet'
lu	'head'
ha	'teeth'
kel	'goat'
wok	'pig'

b. Disyllabic free root:

kedoy	'sheep'
kaŋŋa	'goose'
kiṛki	'parrot'
əma	'he'
pelep	'butterfly'
sinteŋ	'month'
cəkma	'cucumber'
pənco	'brinjal'
simbu	'owl'

C. Polysyllabic free root

wakkəykoŋ	'king fisher'
ritʰaruy	'nerve'
tʰurumiŋ	'story'
kʰasəon	'garlic'
suəncim	'midnight'
tiktiniŋ	'cuckoo'

Bound Roots

In Koireng, limited numbers of bound roots are available. For convenient in analyzing they can be categorized in the following ways:

a. Kinship terms

Examples:

-pa	'father'
-nu	'mother'
-nəynu	'sister (younger)'

-unu	'sister (elder)'
-ne	'father's sister'
-upa	'brother (elder)'
-nəypa	'brother (younger)'
-pu	'brother in law'

To these bound kinship terms pronominal markers **ki-** first person pronominal marker (1pp) or **ni-** the second pronominal marker or **ə–** the third pronominal marker 3pp is added to form a word (to form a complete kinship term). Otherwise it does not give a complete form, as in the following example.

ki-pa	'my father'
ni-pa	'your father'
ə-pa	'his father'(is also used in addressing)

b. Miscellaneous

The following nominal bound roots are to be prefixed by the third person pronominal marker **ə-**, otherwise, it does not give any meaning.

Examples:-

əcon	'duty (his)
ədon	'but (its)
əbuo	'leaf (its)
əhe̥r	'pieces (its)
əmuŋ	'place (its)
ərol	'top(its)
əpḁr	'border(its)

7.2 Affixes

Affixes are bound roots which can only occur attached to a root, or stem or word. In an agglutinative language, affixes are very important. They take part in the formation of various words and in deriving several word class, namely verb, noun, adjective and adverb. Besides these, they are used in forming various sentence types- declarative, negative, interrogative and imperative.

There are two types of affixes i.e. prefix and suffix. Infix is not found in Koireng. They are discussed in the following: -

7.2.1 Prefixes

In Koireng, there are some prefixes. They are (a) pronominal prefix, (b) causative prefix (c) Reflexive prefix, (d) directional prefix, etc. They are discussed below: -

Pronominal Prefix

There are three pronominal prefixes. They **ki-** for fisrt person (1pp), **ni-** for second person (2pp) and **ə–** for third person (3pp). The pronominal prefixes **ki-**, **ni-** and **ə–** are derived from the first person pronoun **kəy** 'I' second person pronoun **nəŋ** 'you' and ə**ma** 'he/she' third person pronoun respectively.

Examples:

(a)	səm	'hair'	ki-səm	'my hair'
	ban	'arm'	ki-ban	'my arm'
	koṛ	'ear'	ki-koṛ	'my ear'
	ke	'feet'	ki-ke	'my feet'
	won	'belly'	ki-won	'my belly'
(b)	lu	'head'	ni-lu	'your head'
	in	'house'	ni-in	'your house'
	koŋ	'waist'	ni-koŋ	'your waist'
	neṛ	'mouth'	ni-neṛ	'your mouth'
	ha	'teeth'	ni-ha	'your teeth'

(c)	may	'face'	ə-may	'his face'
	ləy	'tongue'	ə-ləy	'his tongue'
	nar	'nose'	ə-nar	'his nose'
	pon	'cloth'	ə-pon	'his cloth'
	cəl	'forehead'	ə-cəl	'his forehead'

Causative Prefix

Causative is formed by prefixing a morpheme **min-** to the verb, as shown in the following examples:

ril	'speak'	min-ril	'cause to speak'
pa	'read'	min-pa	'cause to read'
wor̩	'throw'	min-wor̩	'cause to throw'
tan	'run'	min-tan	'cause to run'
in	'drink'	min-in	'cause to eat'
sin	'small'	min-sin	'cause to smaller'
liean	'big'	min-lien	'cause to bigger'
suoy	'cook'	min-suoy	'cause to cook'
sin	'ripe'	min-sin	'cause it to to ripe'

Reflexive Prefix

The prefix **ki-** is used reflexive prefix by adding to the action verb.

Examples:

cak	'eat'	ki-cak	'to eat oneself'
in	'drink'	ki-in	'to drink oneself'
wa	'come'	ki-wa	'to come oneself'
ce	'go'	ki-ce	'to go oneself'
ril	'speak'	ki-ril	'to speak oneself'

en	'look'	kin-en	'to look oneself'
tok	'touch'	ki-tok	'to touch oneself'

Directional Prefix

In this language, the prefix **hoŋ-** is used as a deictic (upward direction) by adding to an action verb. Examples:

tan	'run'	hoŋ-tan	'to run upward'
o	'fly'	hoŋ-o	'to fly upward'
peṛ	'kick'	hoŋ-peṛ	'to kick upward'
heṛ	'turn'	hoŋ-heṛ	'to turn upward'
mu	'look'	hoy-mu	'to look up'
kay	'climb'	hoy-kay	'to climb up'

Besides these prefixes, there are some suffixes which indicate direction. They are discussed in the suffix section.

The prefix **ə–** is also used in the formation of new word i.e. the derived noun. Examples:

kaŋ	'climb'	ə-kaŋ	'climber'
cak	'eat	ə-cak	'eater'
pa	'read'	ə-pa	'reader'
ril	'speak'	ə-ril	'speaker'
tan	'run'	ə-tan	'runner'
t^ho	'do'	ə-t^ho	'doer'

Reciprocal prefix

The prefix **ker-** is used as a reciprocal prefix by adding to the verb. The presence of the reciprocal marker in this language is a distinctive feature of Tibeto-Burman sub-family. The examples are given below:

wok	'beat'	ker-wok	'to beat each other'

ŋo	'quarrel	ker-ŋo	'to quarrel each other'
e	'look'	ker-in	'to look each other'
luŋtʰək	'angry'	ker-luŋtʰək	'to angry each other'
pər	'kick'	kər-pər	'to kick each other'
hər	'turn'	kər-hər	'to turn each other'
mu	'see'	kə-mu	'to see each other'
ril	'speak'	kə-ril	'to speak each other'

7.2.2 Suffixes:

The affixes which can occur after the root are known as suffixes. There are many suffixes which are more than the number of prefixes. Suffixes can be divided into two categories i.e. (a) nominal suffixes and (b) verbal suffixes. They are discussed below:

a. Nominal suffixes

Nominal suffixes are very large in number. They are plural markers, diminutive marker, case markers, demonstrative markers, gender marker etc.

1. Gender Suffixes

There are two different sets of suffixes to indicate male and female: for animal **cəl** and **pi** are used to express male and female respectively; for bird **kʰoŋ** and **pi** are used to express male and female respectively (see for detail in gender)

For expressing common gender a suffix –**te** is used (-**te** indicates small). Examples;

uy-te	'puppy'
se-te	'calf'

2. Number Suffixes

In Koireng, the suffixes –**hay** and –**təm** are used as a number suffix for indicating plural marker and the suffix –**rikip** is used as a collective noun (see for detail in number).

3. Case Suffixes

There are seven case suffixes They are:

Agentive marker	-hin/han
Accusative narker	-hi
Genitive marker	-ta
Intrumental marker	-a ~la ~ŋa ~ ma etc.
Locative marker	- ə~lə~ŋə ~mə etc.
Associative marker	-le
Ablative marker	-taka

(see for detail in Case)

4. Demonstrative Suffixes

The suffixes –**hi** and –**ha** are used as a demonstrative suffix.

Examples;

uy	'dog'	uy-ha	'dog + that'
uy	'dog'	uy-hi	'dog + this'

There are certain suffixes which indicate the place as well as direction. These suffixes indicate the exact location as given below:

-cuŋŋə	'one or above'
-suŋŋə	'in or inside'
-tollə	'out or outside'
-noyyə	'below or under'

Examples:

-cuŋŋə 'on or above'

lu-cuŋŋə	'on or above the head'
tʰiŋ-cuŋŋə	'on or above the tree'
in-cuŋŋə	'on or above the house'
tebəl-cuŋŋə	'on or above the table'
-suŋŋə	'in or inside'
in-suŋŋə	'in or inside the house'
ka-suŋŋə	'in or inside the room'
cepəŋ-suŋŋə	'in or inside the granary'
bubel-suŋŋə	'in or inside the rice pot'
-tollə	'out or outside'
in-tollə	'outside the house'
iskul-tollə	'outside the school'
hol-təllə	'outside the hall'
tukan-tollə	'outside the shop'
-noyyə	'below or under'
tʰiŋ-noyyə	'below/under the tree'
tebəl-noyyə	'below/ under the table'
yamul-noyyə	'below/ under the bed'

Exclusiveness

The suffix –**bəy** is added to a noun to indicate 'only'

Examples:

ən-bəy	'only cury'
ŋa- bəy	'only fish'
cəy-bəy	'only spear'
mici-bəy	'only salt'

Verbal Suffixes

In Koireng, there are some verbal suffixes. They are aspect marker, negative markers, imperative marker, and interrogative markers.

A. Aspect markers

Koireng has four aspect markers they are added to the verb. They are;

Simple aspect	-ɸ (pronominal + verb)
Progressive aspect	-le (pronominal + pro. asp. + verb)
Perfective aspect	-yəy (pronominal + verb + per. asp.)
Unrealised aspect	-te (pronominal + verb + unreal. asp.)
	(see for detail in Aspect)

B. Sentence markers

In Koireng, different types of sentences, such as negation, imperative and interrogative are formed by adding respective markers to the verb as given below: -

Negation-	by adding – **mək/-no/-ləy** markers
Imperative-	by adding –**ro/-ru** markers
Interrogative-	by adding –**mo** marker

(see for detail in respective section)

The conjunct particle **-ə /-yara** 'since', **inko** 'if', **innum** although', **le** 'after', **maceŋ** 'until' etc. are suffixed to the verb. (see for detail in conjunction).

8

Word Formation

8.1 Word Formation

Word formation deals with 'the creation of new words'. It is the process of morphological variation in the constitution of words. In Koireng, word-formation employs two processes i.e. affixation and compounding. They are discussed below: -

8.1.1 Affixation

In affixation, there are two processes for the formation of word i.e. prefixation and suffixation.

Prefixation

In Koireng, there are only one prefix ə– which is added to the root to derive a word. By its prefixation, the word class is changed.

Example: -

Verb	*Noun*
in 'drink'	ə-in 'drinker'
cak 'eat'	ə-cak 'eater'
pa 'read'	ə-pa 'reader'

tan 'run'	ə-tan 'runner'
t^ho 'do'	ə-t^ho 'doer'

The pronominal prefixes i.e. **ki-** first person, **ni-**second person and ə–third person are used in kinship reference as well as addressing terms.

Example: -

pa	'father'		
ki+pa	>	kipa	'my father'
ni+pa	>	nipa	'your father'
ə+pa	>	əpa	'his father'

These pronominal prefixes are also used in referring to the body parts.

Example: -

ban 'arm'	ki+ban	>	kiban 'my hair'
won 'belly'	ni+won	>	niwon 'your belly'
kut 'hand'	ə+kut	>	əkut 'his hand'

The prefix **əni-**is used for making 'manner of' .Examples are given below:

ril 'speak'	əni-ril	'manner of speaking'
cak 'eat'	əni-cak	'manner for eating'
tan 'run'	əni-tan	'manner of running'
pa 'read'	əni-pa	'manner of reading'
to 'do'	əni-to	'manner of doing'

There are also some suffixes which involved the word formation. They are gender markers (**-cəl** 'male' and **-pi** 'female') and diminutive suffix –**te**.

Example:

-cəl 'male' –**pi** 'female'

serat+cəl	>	seratcəl	'bull'
serat+pi	>	seratpi	'cow'
selo+cəl	>	selocəl	'buffalo(M)'
selo+pi	>	selopi	'buffalo(F)'

Diminutive marker –**te** 'small'

Examples:

uy+te	>	uyte	'puppy'
pasəl+te	>	pasəlte	'boy'(small)
numəy+te	>	numəyte	'girl'(small)

8.1.2 Compounding

It is the formation of new words in which words are formed by the combination of two or more roots. It may be the combination of noun + noun, noun + verb, noun + adjective, etc. They are discussed in the following: -

Noun + Noun

It is the formation of nouns with the combination of another two nouns.

Examples:

se + ek	>	se-ek	'cow dung'
cow dung			
mit + mul	>	mit-mul	'eyelash'
eye body hair			
əncəm + riek	>	əncəm-riek	'mustard oil'
mustard oil			

Noun + Adjective

It is the formation of nouns derived from the combination of a noun and an adjective.

Examples:

uy +te	>	uyte	'puppy'
dog small			
se + te	>	sete	'calf'
cow small			
pasəl + te	>	pasəlte	'boy'(small)
man small			
numəy + te	>	numəyte	'girl'
woman small			
kum +t^{h}əṛ	>	kumt^{h}əṛ	'New year'
year new			
kum + luy	>	kumluy	'last year
year last			

Noun +Verb

In this compound, it is also the formation of nouns with the combination of a noun and a verb.

Examples: -

pon + koŋ	>	ponkoŋ	'weaver'
cloth weave			
ləy + tho	>	ləytho	'farmer'
paddy plant work			
in + sək	>	insək	'house maker'(builder)
house make			

On the basis of semantics, compounding may be divided into three types. They are: - (I) endocentric compounds (II) exocentric compound (III) coordinate compounds

8.1.2.1 Endocentric Compounds

There are two types of endocentric compounds i. e. Right-headed compounds and left headed compounds.

Right-headed compounds

In this compounds, both the constituents are generally found to be nominal bases. The two nouns might be related with one another either by the possessive suffix –**ta** or by one of the several bases that are not actually related in the final composite word.

Examples are given below: -

wa-ta əneṛ 'beak of bird' > waneṛ 'beak'

bird-GEN-beak

t^hiŋ-ta əbuo 'leaf of tree' > t^hiŋbuo 'leaf'

tree-GEN-leaf

məy-ta əri 'string of flame > məyi 'flame'

fire-GEN-string

ke-ta əbiye 'print of foot' > kibiye 'foot print'

foot-GEN-print

There is another type of possessive relationship that of directional, as in the following examples:

mit-ta əbor > mitbor 'eyelid'

eye-GEN. border

pon-ta əbor > ponbor 'lace'

cloth-GEN. border

mit-ta əlay > mitlay 'centre of eye'

eye-GEN. middle

kut-ta əlay	>	kutlay	'middle finger'
hand-GEN. middle			
mit-ta ənoy	>	mitnoy	'bottom of eye'
eye-GEN. gottom			

Verbal Relation: In this types of right-headed compound underlying structure is of syntactic one, that is showing their relationship in a syntachic structure. Examples:

ṛəm-mə om uy	>	ṛəmuy	'fox'
land-DET live dog			
ən suoŋ bel	>	ənbel	'curry pot'
curry cook pot			
in-nə om sa	>	insa	'domestic animal'
house-DET. live animal			

There are some other right-headed compound having the noun(substantive) root **nəmun** 'place' as the second constituent element and an action oriented root as the first element.

Examples:-

suoŋ +nəmun	>	suoŋnəmun	'kitchen'
cook place			
suy +nəmun	>	suynəmun	'tailoring place'
stitch place			(tailoring house)
yor + nəmun	>	yonəmun	'selling place'
sell place			(shop)
tak +nəmun	>	taknəmun	'falling place'
fall place			
om + nəmun	>	omnəmun	'accomodation
live place			

en + nəmun > ennəmun ' watching place'

Left-headed Compound

In the left-headed compounds, the second constituent element as the head, is a noun. The compounds are formed by reversing the order of the underlying structure and simultaneously root of the first element is retained as in the following examples:

ələmlək mi > milələmlək 'stranger'

strange man

əsəy ro > rosəy 'the whole bamboo'

long bamboo

əthəṛ mi > mithəṛ 'new person'

new man (new shelter)

ərik p^hur > p^huṛrik 'load'

heavy object

əpak ṛəm > ṛəmpak 'play ground'

broad land

əsen po > ponsen 'red cloth'

red cloth

ət^hi t^ha > t^hat^hi 'new moon'

dead moon

əp^hun t^hiŋ > t^hip^hun 'post'

erected tree

əlien mi > milien 'big man'

big man

əlien luŋ > luŋlien 'rock'

big stone

8.1.2.2 Exocentric Compound

In Koireng, exocentric compounds are generally made up of a nouns or nouns and adverbial root. Both the noun and the verbal root cannot be regarded as a head or the attribute in this compound.

Examples: -

kay kəl nəyna	>	kaŋkəl	'mosquito net'
mosquito prevent thing			
mol tum nəyna	>	mol tum	'pillow cover'
pillow cover thing			
ha əy nət	>	haəy	'teeth ache'
teeth ache disease			
lu hay nət	>	luhay	'vertigo'
head mad disease			

There are some other exocentric compound in which the noun **mi** 'man' is functioning as a covert head as exemplified below: -

luŋ t^{h}o mi	>	luŋ t^{h}o	'manson'
stone work man			
ləy t^{h}o mi	>	ləyt^{h}o	'farmer'
paddy plant work man			
pon k^{h}oŋ mi	>	ponk^{h}oŋ	'weaver'
cloth weave man			
in sək mi	>	insək	'builder'
house make man			
t^{h}iŋ t^{h}o mi	>	t^{h}iŋt^{h}o	'carpenter'
tree work man			

8.1.3 Co-ordinate Compound

In this type of compound, both the elements function jointly as head which are generally of two different nouns joined together through a conjunction suffix –**le.**

Examples:-

in-le ləl-le	>	inləl	'property'
house and wealth			
bu-le ən-le	>	buən	'meal'
rice and curry			
əca-le ətu-le	>	əcaətu	'issues'
(his)son and (his) grand son			
cəy-le cəm-le	>	cəycəm	'weapon'
spear and knife			
ca-ŋle cəcay-le	>	caŋəcay	'paddy and rice'
paddy and rice			
mit-le koṛ-le	>	mitkoṛ	'eye and ear'
eye and ear			
$buk^{h}e$ŋ-le $ənk^{h}e$ŋ-le	>	$buk^{h}e$ŋ$ənk^{h}e$ŋ	'plate and bowl'
plate and bowl			

9

Sentence Structures

9.1 Sentence Structures

On the structural basis sentence, it can be analysed into three types. They are (i) Simple sentence. (ii) Complex sentence and (iii) Compound sentence.

9.1.1 Simple Sentence

In the simple sentence, there is only one verb. It remarks a simple statement (expressing habitual, natural truth or routine action).

Examples:

1 kəy tuy ki-in

---I water 1pp.-drink

'I drink water.'

2 nəŋ tuy ni-in

you water 2pp.-drink

'You drink water.'

3 əma tuy ə–in

he water 3pp.-drink

'He drinks water.'

Koireng is a verbal pronominalized language, that is, the pronominal prefixes **ki-**, **ni-**, and **ə–** are (the first person, second person and third person pronominal prefixes are respectively) prefixed to the verb. (see for detail in Declarative sentence).

9.1.2 Complex Sentence

A complex sentence consists of at least a matrix clause and one or more dependent clause, they are connected by the conjunctive particles namely, **hawahako** 'that' **maceŋ** 'until' **-ə/-yara** 'since' **inko** 'if', **əninum** 'though', **le** 'after' etc.

Examples;

4. kəy-hin ki-t^{h}əydəŋ hawahako əma ce-ə-te
   I-NOM. 1pp-know that he go-3pp-UNRE.
   'I know that he will go.'

5. kəy wa-maceŋ əma-hin ə–wom
   I come-until he-NOM. 3pp-live
   'He stayed on until I arrived.'

6. əma ə–nay-yara iskul ce-mək-e
   he 3pp.-ill-since school go-NEG-PART
   'He does not go to school since he is ill.'

7. əma ə–hoŋ-inko kəy iskul ce-ki-te
   he 3pp.-come-if I school go-3pp.UNRE
   'If he comes I will go to school.'

8 əma ki-məl-əninum kəy-hin əma sən-no-niŋ
  he 1pp.-friend-though I-NOM. he help-NEG-NEGUN-PART
  'Though he is my friend, I will not support him.'

9 əma ə–yoŋ-le kəy ki-ce

he 3pp.-come-after I 1pp.-go

'After he comes I also go.'

9.1.3 Compound Sentence

There are two or more independent clauses which are connected with the help of coordinating conjunction, namely, **hənko** 'and', **hawayara / hawarin** 'therefore' **yəytək** 'but' **əniraŋŋata** 'even though', etc.

Examples;

10. əma koy-ro hənko larik min-pa-ro

he call-COMD.mk. and book CAUS.mk-read-COMD.mk.

'Call him and make him read the book'.

11. kəy bu cə-mək-iŋ hawayara kəy iskul ce-no-niŋ

I rice eat-NEG.-PART. therefore I school go-NEG.U-com.

'I don't eat rice therefore I will no go school.'

12. kəy pon som-ki-te yəytək əma bu suoŋ-ə-te

I cloth wash-1pp.-UNRE. but he rice cook-3pp-UNRE.

'I shall wash cloth but he will cook rice.'

13. tombə cuon ninəktəkka ə–tʰo əniraŋŋata əma hoytʰəy-mək-e

Tomba work hard 3pp.-do even though he happy NEG.-PART

'Tomba work hard even though he is not happy.'

14. tombə ə–ker˥coŋ yəytak əma hoytʰəy-mək-e

Tomba 3pp.-rich but he happy-NEG.-PART

'Tomba is a rich person but he is not happy.'

9.1.4 Conjunction

The words which join the clauses, phrases or words are treated as conjunctions. It can help in conveying a complete meaning of a construction. In English the words like **and**, **but** or **therefore**, etc. are conjunct words. Today the trem **conjuction** is normally applied to a very small group of words, mainly **and** and **or**, which were traditionally called the **coordinating conjunctions** most usually, a conjunction **conjoins** (joins) two or more instances of the same category. For instance: **would you like a chocolate or a a pice of pie?** (conjoned nown phrases); **John finished his dinner, lit a cigarette and started his walk** (conjoned verb phases).

Traditional grammarians also included among the conjunctions another group, the **subordinating conjunctions** or subordinators, for examples, **if, wherever, although** and **after,** which introduce adverbial caluses. Examples: **After she arrives in time she can meet us**. But these words behave very differently from the true conjunctions, and today they are normally placed in a class by themselves.

In Koireng, there are a number of words which are used as conjunction. They are as follows;

le-le	'and or with'
yum	'also'
ə/yara	'since'
inko	'if'
innum	'although'
hənako	'and then'
həwayara / hawarin	'therefore'
ənimәkle	'either or'
ənirəŋŋata	'eventhough'
yəytak	'even then'
əyarko	'because' etc.

Conjunct particle *le-le* 'and' or 'with'

This conjunct particle is added to each noun or to each pronoun occurred in the sentence as exemplified below:

15. tombə-le cawbə-le ce-ən-te

    Tomba-and. chaoba-and. go-3pp-UNRE.

    'Tomba and Chaoba will go.'

16. kəy-le əma-le wa-kin-te

    I-and. he-and. come-1pp.-unreal.asp.

    'I will come with him.'

17. tombə-le cawbə-le kay-le

    Tomba-and chaoba-and I-and

    ce-an-te go-3pp-UNRE

    'Tomba chaoba and I will go'

    (I and he will come)

It is seen that the conjunction particle is added to each nouns or pronouns in the construction.

Conjunct particle yum 'also'

This conjunct particle is added to the noun like the conjunct particle **le-le** and the conjunction particle is added to each nouns and pronouns. Examples;

17. Tomba-yum Jimy-yum Iskul-lə ce-kin-te

    I-also he-also go-1pp.-UNRE.

    'Tomba and Jimy also will go to school'

18. kəy-yum əma-yum wa-kin-te

    I-also he-also come-1pp-UNRE.

    'I and he will come.'

From the above two sentences it is seen that to all nouns/pronouns the conjunctive particle **–yum** is found added.

Conjunct particle -ə/-yara 'since'

The conjunct particle **-ə/-yara** 'since' is added to the verb as exemplified below:

19. kəy ki-na-ə bu cə-mək-iŋ
    I 1pp.-ill-since rice eat-NEG.-PART.
    'Since I am ill, I don't eat rice.'

20. əma-hin ə–t^hem-ə larik-hi ə–cet-yəy
    he-NOM. 3pp.-hold-since book-DET. 3pp-tear-PERF.
    'Since he holds the book, the book has torn.'

Conjunct particle *inko* 'if'

The conjunct particle **inko** 'if' is added to the verb, for instance;

21. nəŋ ni-ce-inko kəy ce-ki-te
    you 2pp.-go-if I go-1pp.-UNRE.
    'If you go, I will go.'

22. əma ə–wa-inko kəy ce-ki-te
    he 3pp.-come-if I go-1pp-UNRE
    'If he comes, I will go.'

Conjunct particle *innum* 'although'

The conjunct particle **innum** 'although' is added to the verb, as given below:

23. əma bu ə–cak-innum ə–won dil-mək-e
    he rice 3pp.-eat-although 3pp-belly swell-NEG-PART
    'Although he eats rice, his belly does not coming up.'

Conjunt word *hnako* 'and then'

It can conjunct phrases and clauses as in the following sentences;

24. bu ca-ro hənako iskul ce-ro

rice eat-COMD. and then school go-COMD.

'(You) eat rice and then go to school'

25. nəŋ ce-ro hənnako waykʰət wa-nol-ro

you go-COMD. and then again come-return-COMD.

'You go and then come again.'

Conjunct word həwayara / hawarin 'therefore'

It is used as a connector of sentences in Koireng as exemplified below:

26. əma yu ə–in hawayara kəy-hin əma niŋsei-mək-iŋ

he liquor 3pp-drink therefore I-NOM. he love-NEG.-PART.

'He drinks liquor therefore I don't love him.'

27. kəy bu ca-mək-iŋ hawayara kəy iskul ce-no-niŋ

I rice eat-NEG.-PART. therefore I school go-NEG-PART

'I don't eat rice therefore I will not go to school.'

Conjunct word ə*nimək*le 'either or'

The conjunct word **ənimәkle** 'or' can connect the nouns or clauses, for instance;

28. nəŋ ənimәkle tombə ce-ro

you or tomba go-COMD

'Either you or Tomba go.'

29. nəŋ iskul ce-ro ənimәkle larik pa-ro

you school go-COMD. or book read-COMD.

'Either you go to school or read the book.'

Conjunct word *ənirəŋŋata* 'even though'

In Koireng, it is used to join clauses as exemplified below;

30. tombə cuon ninəktəkkə ə–tʰo ənirəŋŋata əma hoytʰəy-mək-e

Tomba work hard 3pp-do even though he happy-NEG.-NCP

'Tomba word hard even though he is not happy.'

31. tombə bu ətəmmə ə–cak ənirəŋŋata ə–won dil-mək-e

Tomba rice very 3pp-eat even though 3pp-belly swell-NEG.-PART

'Tomba eats rice very much even though his belly is not coming up.'

Conjunct word yəytak 'even than'

It is used to connect two sentences or clauses.

32. tombə ə–keṛcoŋ yəytak əma hoytʰəy-mək-e

Tomba 3pp.-rich even than he happy-NEG-NCP

'Tomba is rich even than he is not happy.'

Conjunct word *əyarko* 'because'

The conjunction **əyarko** 'because' is used to connect phrase or clause as exemplified below:

33. kəy təl ca-no-niŋ əyarko kəy bu ca-ki-te

I bread eat-ft.NEG. because I rice eat-1pp.-UNRE

I will not eat bread because I will eat rice.'

34. naypəŋ-ha keṛday-no-niə əyarko əma larik pa-ə-te

child-ddet. play-ft.NEG.UN because he book read-3pp.-UNRE

'The child will not play because he will read book.'

9.1.5 Cansativization

A causatrive construction indicates a situation in which two events are involved: a preceding causing event and a subsequent caused event.

They occur in such a way that if there how been no causing event, the caused event could not have followed. This situation is called 'macrosituation' which is thus comprised of two microsituation: a causing microsituation or antecedent and a caused microsituation or consequent.

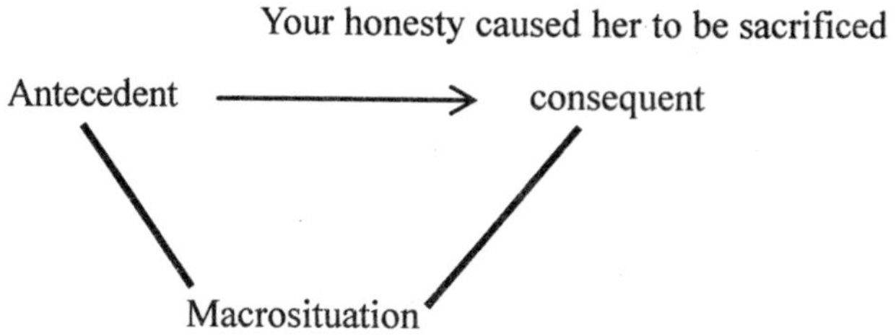

The causing microsituation is 'your honesty' as consequence of which 'she was sacrificed'. It can be asserted that had you not been honesty she would not have been worried.

Causative forms are of two types morphologically regular and productive forms, and non-productive forms which are morphologically irregular. Productive causative constructions involved either the use of auxiliary causative verbs or the use of affixes. Languages of the isolation type have a tendency to use auxiliary causative verbs while agglutinative languages tend to use affixes.

In koireng causativization is done through the process of preffixation of the causative marker **min-** to the verb, at the same time the verbal prominalization also takes place. The examples are given below:

35.a). əmán larik-ha ə-nuk-ther
he-AGNT book-DET 3ppt tear
'He tears the book'

b). əma-n thoibi-hi tark khət ə-min-nukther
he-AGNT Thoibi-ACC book one 3pp-CAUS-tear
'HE causes Thoibi tear one book'

36.a). kəi kəithel-lə ki-ce

I market-LOC 1pp-go

'I go to market'

b). ənmani-hin kəi-hi kəithel-la market-LOC

they-AGNT I-ACC əni-min-ce 3pp-CAUS-go

ən-mani-hi the they bre mrkhoi

'They cause me go to market'

37. əma-han ə-pon ə-in-boŋ

he-AGNT his-cloths 3pp-CAUS-white

'He whitens his clothes'

38.a). əma-hin kəi-hi əbi-wok

he-AGNT i-ACC 3pp-beat

'He beats me'

b). əma-hin kəi-hi əni-̀min-wok

he-AGNT I-ACC 3pp-CAUS-beat

'He causes someone beat me'

The causative marker **min-** is very productive it (**min-**) can be added to any verb for the causative formation. Examples:

ce 'go' min-ce causing somebody go (prog)

in 'drink' min-in cause somebody drink

suoŋ 'cook' minsuoŋ 'perfect'

cook

Lexical Causatives

sibə - 'die' -əthi hat-pə 'kill' ə-hət

ca-bə - 'eat'-əcak pijəbə 'feed'-min-ak

thrk-pə - 'drink'-əin	pi-thəkpə- 'feed' (liquid)-minin
tumbə - 'sleep'-ə̀in	sumbə- 'full' – oi-in (min-in)
yeŋbə- 'see'-en	ut-pə- 'show'-min-mu
məi-caupə-to catch- məi-kaŋ	məi-thabə- 'burn'-məi-hal

fire

təu-bə 'dig' cəI	phumbə-'bury'-phum
Rəu-bə 'take'-ləI	mət-pə 'confisticate'-su-ol
	munbə 'snatch'
kaibə- 'break'-ə-koi	thugaibə 'lomaka' to make it broken-mikhoi
tət-pə 'to break-kertən	thəthət-pə̀-to make the thread or
	wirè potən 'break'

9.1.6 Copula

The copula **ni** takes the respetive pronominal markers **ki-, ni-** and **ə-** in singular number and for the plural it (**ni**) takes **kin-, nin-** and **ən-** for the repective plural number. The examples are: (a: for singular, b: for plural).

39. a)	kəy	tombə	ki-ni
	I	Tomba	1pp-COP
	'I am Tomba'		
b)	kəy-ni	dəktər	kin-ni
	I-PL	docter	1pp-COP
	'We are doctors'		
40. a)	nəŋ	ləwmi	ə-ni
	you	farmer	3pp-COP
	'you are a farmer'		

b) nəŋ-ni ləwmi nin-ni

you-PL farmer 2pp-COP

You are farmers'

41. a) əma niŋsək ə-ni

he thief 3pp-COP

'He is a thief'

b) ənmani niŋsək ən-ni

they thief 3pp-COP

'They are thieves'

In this language the copula is treated as a word because it (ni) takes its respective prominal prefixes **ki-, ni-** and **ə-** for singular pronouns while **kin-, nin-** and **ən** for the plural pronouns. In sentence (39) the 1st pronominal prefix **ki-**(singular) and **kin-**(pl) are prefixed to the copula according to the number. In the same way the sentence (40a) and (b) show for the second persons the respective pronominal prefixes **ni** (singular) and **nin** (plural) are prefixed to the copula. For the third person subject, in sentence (41a) and (b) the respective pronominal prefixes **ə-** and ən- are prefixed to the copula **ni**. Some more examples are given here:

42. daktər-ha pasəl ə-ni

doctor-DET boy 3pp-COP

'That doctor is a bachelor (man)'

43. kəy-ni unay səri kin-ni

I-PL sibling seven 1pp-COP

'We are seven sibling'

44. pasəl-te-ha kinthum-suna ə-ni

boy-small-DET three-ORD 3pp-COP

'That boy is the third one'

10

Sentence Process

10.1 Declarative Sentence

Declerative sentence shows the word order of the language. Koireng is a verbal pronominalized language as exemplified below:

1. kəy bu ki-cak

   I rice 1pp.-eat

   'I eat rice.'

2. nəŋ bu ni-cak

   you rice 2pp.-eat

   'You eat rice.'

3. əma bu ə–cak

   he rice 3pp.-eat

   'He eats rice.'

4. tomba bu-ə-cak

   'Tomba eats rice'

5. kəy-ni thiy əsay əsay ki-tuk

   I – PL tree tall tall Ipp-cut

   'We cut tall trees'

6. ənma-ni thing əsay əsay ə-tuk

he-PL tree tall tall -3pp-cut

'They cut tall trees'

The prefixes **ki-** in sentence (1) **ni-** in sentence (2) and **ə-** in sentence (3) are the respective verbal pronominal markers of respective persons, i.e., first person **kəy** 'I', second person **nŋ** 'you' and third person **əma** 'he'. The process of affixation, here it is of prefixation, of the respective personal marker to the verb is regarded as regarded as verbal pronominalization. This type of grammatical feature is generally found in Kuki groups of languages. This grammatical features is found in declarative construction not only in negative, introgative and imperative. The respective pronominal markers are also used in plural as in sentences (8) and (9).

The declarative sentence shows the word order of a language. Koireng is a subject – object - verb (SOV) word order. In another word, Koireng is a verb final language. The above three sentences also show it.

(a) Numeral follows the noun as in sentence (7)

7.	əma	t^həyhay	riŋŋa	ə–cak
	he	mango	five	3pp.-eat

'He eats five mango.'

(b) Adjctive follows the noun as in (8)

8.	əma	t^həyhay	lien	kink^{h}ət	ə-cak
	he	mango	big	one	3pp.-eat

'He eats a big mango.'

(c) Determiner follows the noun, as in (9)

9.	kəy	soŋkol-hi	ki-dəy
	I	shirt-DET	1pp.-like

'I like this shirt.'

(d) Adverb precedes the verb as in (10)

10. əma əyaŋ-təkkə ə–ce
    he fast-acc. 3pp.-go
    'He goes very fast.'

Koireng is a postposition language. The following examples substantiate the statement.

11. larik-ha tebəl-cuŋŋə ə-om
    book-ddet table-on 3pp.-stay
    'The book is on the table.'

12. əma in-suŋŋə ə-om
    he house-inside 3pp.-live
    'He stays inside the house.'

13. kəy hol-tollə ə-suok
    I hall-outside 3pp.-move
    'I go outside the hall.'

14. kolom-ha tebəl-noyyə ə–om
    pen-DET. table-under 3pp.-live
    'The pen is under the table.'

15. soŋkol-ha tebəl-sirrə ə-om
    shirt-DET table-border 3pp.-live
    'The shirt is border the table.'

Koireng has case markers which are all suffixed to the noun (see for detail in case.).

10.2 Negation

All human sytems of communication contain a representation of negation. Negation, no doubt, still occupies the crossroads of developments in linguistic theory, the psychologists, the philosophy of language and mind, and the history of ideas. Its comptex behaviour in lexical incorporations (**impossible,** can't detain) provides vital data on the nature of constraints of word formation.

There are different devices for different languages to convert affirmative construction to negative construction. Some languages employ separate negative lexeme before and after the verb; in some languages it is done by addition of affixes to the verb. Koireng uses affixal stretagy for negative formation. In Koireng, thre are three negative, markers. They are given below:

In Koireng, there are three types of negative markers. They are given below:

(i) –**mək** used in realized aspect /non future.

(ii) –**no** used in unrealized aspect /furure

(iii) –**ləy** used in the morphological level.

10.3 Negative Concord particles

Koireng has concord particles occurring with the first person, second person and third person, that is, **-iŋ** occurs with first person singular and **uŋ** with the first person plural; **-ci** occurs with the second person singular and **ciu** with the second person plural; **e** occurs with third person singular and **u** with third person plural; in the formation of realized negation.

Examples:

(A) Realised Negation

16. kəy bu cə-mək-iŋ
    I rice eat-NEG-NCP
    'I do not take rice'

17. əyni bu cə-mək-uŋ
    we rice eat-NEG-NCP
    'We do not take rice'

18. nəŋ bu cə-mək-ci
you rice eat-NEG-NCP
'You do not take rice'

19. nəŋni bu cə-mək-ciu
you(pl.) rice eat-NEG-NCP
'You do not take rice.'

20. əma bu cə-mək-e
he rice eat-NEG-NCP
'He do not take rice'

21. ənmani bu cə-mək-u
they rice eat-NEG-NCP
'They do not take rice'

The particle **niŋ** occurs with the first person singular and **məni** with the first person plural; **tini** occurs with the second person singular and **tiniu** with the second person plural; **-ni** occurs with the person singular and **niu** with third person plural in the formation of unrealized negation.

Unrealised Negation

22. kəy bu cə-no-niŋ
I rice eat-NEG-NCP
'I shall not eat rice'

23. əyni bu cə-no-məni
we rice eat-NEG. NCP
'We shall not eat rice'

24. nəŋ bu cə-no-niti
you rice eat-NEG-NCP
'You will not eat rice'

25. nəŋni bu cə-no-tiniu
you(pl) rice eat-NEG-NCP
'you(pl) will not eat rice'

26. əma bu cə-no-ni
he rice eat-NEG-NCP
'He will not eat rice'

27. ənmani bu cak-no-niu
they rice eat-NEG-NCP
'They will not eat rice.'

10.4 Negative markers

(i) –mək

The negative marker –**mək** is used in the non-future sentences. which is expressing the habitual sense. It is followed by the concord particle, denying an action happening in the past (past action). The pronominal prefixes, such as **ki-**, **ni-** and **ə–** for the first person, second person and third person respectively are deleted in the negative formation.

Example:

28. a.kəy yu ki-in
I liquor 1pp.-drink
'I drink liquor.'

b. kəy yu in-mək-iŋ
I liquor drink-NEG-NCP
'I don't drink liquor.'

29. a. nəŋ iskul ni-ce
you school 2pp.-go
'You go to school.'

b. nəŋ iskul ce-mək-ci
you school go-NEG-NCP
'You don't go to school.'

30. a. əma naypəŋ ə-ni
he child 3pp.-be
'He is a child.'

b. əma naypəŋ ni-mək-e
he child be-NEG.NCP
'He is not a child.'

(ii) –no

The negative marker –**no** expresses the meaning of futurity and it is followed by the concord particle - **niŋ**. The pronominal prefixes are deleted in the formation of negative as exemplified below:

31. a. kəy iskul ce-ki-te
I school go-1pp.UNRE
'I will go to school.'

b. kəy iskul ce-no-niŋ
I school go.NEG-NCP
'I will not go to school.'

32. a. əma serinutuy in-ə-te
he milk drink-3pp-UNRE
'He will drink milk.'

b. əma serinutuy in-no- niŋ
he milk drink-NEG-NCP
'He will not drink milk.'

(iii) -ləy

The negative marker –**ləy** is used in the morphological level, as given below:

33. a. ə–əm naypəŋ
    Fp-fool child
    'Foolish child'

    b. əm-ləy naypəŋ
    fool-NEG child
    'Clever child

34. a. ə–luŋtʰək mi
    Fp.-angry man
    'angry man'

    b. luŋtʰək-ləy mi
    angry-NEG. man
    'Gentleman

35. a. ə–ciŋ mi
    Fp.-wise man
    'Wise man'

    b. ciŋ-ləy mi
    wise-NEG. man
    'Unwise man'

Prohibitive

In Koireng, prohibitive is formed by the suffixation of negative marker –**mək** to the verbal root. In this prohibitive the command marker –**ro** is used for singular and the command marker–**ru** is used for plural as exemplified below:

36. a. nəŋ ce-ro

you go-COMD.

'You go.'

b. nəŋ ce-mək-ro

you go-NEG-COMD.

'Don't go.'

37. a. nəŋ-ni ce-ru

you-pl. go-COMD.

'Go.'(pl)

b. nəŋ-ni ce-mək-ru

you-pl. go-NEG-COMD.

'Don't go.'(pl)

38. yu in-mək-ro

Liquor drink-NEG-COMD

'Don't drink liquor'

'Let' Negative

In Koireng, 'let' negative is formed by combination of negative marker –**mək** and the proposal marker –**roy** which is suffixed to the verbal roots after the negative marker as given below:

39. a. əyni bu ca-roy

we rice eat-Let

'Let us eat rice.'

b. əyni bu ca-mək-roy

we rice eat-NEG-Let

'Let us not eat rice.'

40. a. əyni yu in-roy

we liquor drink-Let

'Let us drink liquor.'

b. əyni yu in-mək-roy

we liquor drink-NEG-Let

'Let us not drink liquor.'

Negative Strengthening

In most of the languages, negative is strengthened through some additional words, such as *never*, *at all* in English. In French, the normal form for negation has been strengthened by the accrual of post verbal elements like **mic** 'crump' point 'a point' especially **pas** 'a step'. In Koireng, negative is strengthened by the suffixation –**lek** to the verbal root which are followed by the negative marker –**mək** and the concord particle. Examples:

41. kəy yu in-lek-mək-iŋ

I liquor drink-never-NEG-NCP

'I never drink liquor.'

42. əma əniləycuoŋ ṛil-lek-mək-e

he lie speak-never-NEG-NCP

'He never tells a lie.'

43. əyni sa tʰət-lek-mək-uŋ

we animal kill-never-NEG-NCP

'We never kill animal.'

Double Negation

In mathematics and algebra, there is a principle or formula that two negatives become a positive. But language is not mathematics. What can be applied to mathematics cannot be applied to language.

Whenever two negatives really refers to the same idea or word the result is invariably positive. However, the negative donnot exactly cancel each other: the longer the expression is always weaker. Double negation, generally in various languages, is used preferably in literary expression.

In Koireng, double negation is formed by adding the negative marker –**ləy** to the verb and the negative marker –**mək** which is suffixed to the formative particle **ni-** as exemplified below:

44. kəy in-ləy ni-mək-iŋ

I drink-NEG. FP-NEG-NCP

'It is not that I don't drink.'

45. nəŋ wa-ləy ni-mək-ci

you come-NEG. FP-NEG-NCP

'It is not that you don't come.'

46. əma ce-ləy ni-mək-e

he go-NEG FP.-NEG-NCP

'It is not that he doesn't go.'

10.5 Imperative

As a general feature imperative sentence has three features (a) underlying of subject, (b) second person being underlying subject and (c) futurity. In imperative there are three types, namely, command, request and 'Let' imperative. Pragmatically, in Koireng, they are found different: command is generally used to the juniors while request is used to the seniors and strangers. 'Let' imperative is generally used in making a suggestion. They are discussed below:

Command

In Koireng, command is constructed by the suffixation of the command marker –**ro** for the singular and –**ru** for the plural to the verbal roots; it can be mentioned here that /u/ indicates plural while / O/ for singular.

47. nəŋ ce-ro

you go-COMD.

'You go.'

48. nəŋ-ni hoŋ-ru

you-pl. come-COMD.

'You(pl) come.'

Request

It is formed through the suffixation of –**pek** to the verbal roots and is followed by the command marker –**r(o)** for singular and –**r(u)** for plural. In this case the pronominal prefixes will be presented as given below:

49. (nəŋ) seratnutuy-hi ni-in-pek-ro

you milk-DET 2pp-drink-REQ-COMD.

'Please (you) drink the milk.

50. (nəŋ) hiwahin ni-hoŋ-pek-ro

you here 2pp-come-REQ-COMD.

'Please (you) come here.'

Prohibitive Command

It is formed through the suffixation of negative marker –**mək** to the verbal roots and it is followed by the command marker –**r(o)** for singular and –**r(u)** for plural. Examples;

51. (nəŋ) ce-mək-ro

you go-NEG-COMD.

'(you) Don't go.'

52. (nəŋ-ni) tan-mək-ru

you-pl. run-NEG-COMD.

'(you) Don't run.'

'Wish' imperative:

'Wish' imperatives are constructed through the suffixation **–rise** and **–riseu** to the verbal roots or stems. Generally such types of sentences are used for those having third person subjects. The suffixes **–rise** and **–riseu** are used when the subjects are third person singular and third person plural respectively. Here also in **–riseu** command marker /u/ indicates plural.

Examples:

53. patʰien-hin əma-ha niŋsiet-rise

God-NOM he-DET love-W.IMP

'May God love him.'

54. patʰien-hin ənmani-ha ŋaydəm-riseu

God-nom. they-ddet bless-W.IMP

'May God bless them.'

Remote Imperative

In Koireng, remote imperative is to perform an action at a distance place (away from the speaker). It is formed by adding **wa-** 'come' and **–r(o)** 'command marker' to the verbal roots. The morpheme – **wa-** is used as a prefixation and **–r(o)** is used as a suffixation as exemplified below:-

55. nəŋ wa-en-ro

you come–look–COMD.

'You go and look.'

56. nəŋ wa-in-ro

you come-drink-COMD.

'You go and drink.'

Permission Imperative

It is also formed by adding the command marker **–r(o)** (for singular) and **–r(u)** (for plural) to the verbal roots or stem.

Examples:-

57. nəŋ-hin dəy-jet ləy-ro

you-NOM like-all take-COMD.

'Take whatever you like.'

58. nəŋ-ni-hin dəy-jet rico-ru

you-pl.-NOM like-all buy-COMD.

'Buy whatever you like.'

Condition Imperative

Condition imperatives are constructed through the suffixation of the command marker –**r(o)** for singular and –**r(u)** for plural **-to** the verbal roots. It has two independent clauses with a connecter **ənniməkkinho** 'otherwise' as exemplified below:-

59. ce-ro ənniməkkinko kəy-hin nəŋ wuok-ki-te

go-COMD. otherwise I-NOM you beat-1pp-UNRE

'Go, otherwise I will beat you.'

60. wa-ro ənniməkkinko kəy-hin pəysa pe-no-niŋ

come-COMD. otherwise I-NOM money give-NEG-NCP

'Come, otherwise I will not give money.'

'Let' request

It is formed by the prefixation of the causative marker **min-** to the verb and the imperative marker –**r(o)** (for singular) and –**r(u)** (for plural) are suffixed to the verb.

Examples:

61. kəy-hi min-ce-ro

I-ACC CAUS-go-COMD

'Let me go please.'

62. ənmani-hi min-ce-mək-ru

they-ACC CAUS-go-NEG-COMD.

'Let them not go please.'

'Let' Imperative

It is an indirect command. 'Let' imperative is used with the first person or third person subjects.

A. 'Let' with the first person singular positive:

The command marker –**r(o)** and the causative marker –**min** are used with a particle –**ni** to express the desire of doing an action and taking the addressee's permission for doing the action.

Examples:

63. kəy ni-min-in-ro

I FP-CAUS-drink-COMD.

'Let me drink.'

64 kəy ni-min-ce-ro

I FP-CAUS-go-COMD.

'Let me go.'

B. 'Let' with a first person singular negative

It is formed with the negative marker –**mək,** the command marker –**r(o)** which is added to the verb, the particle **ni-** and the causative marker **min-** are also added to the verb as exemplified below:

65. kəy la nim-min-t^{h}o-mək-ro

I song FP-CAUS-sing-NEG-COMD.S

'Let me not sing the song.'

66. kəy ni-min-ce-mək-ro

I FP-CAUS-go-NEG-COMD.

'Let me not go.'

C. 'Let' with a first person plural positive

In this case, 'Let' imperative gives the meaning of suggestion both to the hearer and speaker. It is formed by adding –**roy** after the verbal roots or stems.

Examples:

67. əyni ce-roy

we go-Let

'Let us go.'

68. əyni in-roy

we drink-Let

'Let us drink.'

D. 'Let' with a first person plural negative

It is formed with the negative marker –**mək** which is suffixed to the verbal roots or stems just before the suggestive marker –**roy** as exemplified below:

69. əyni oŋ-mək-roy

we sit-NEG-Let

'Let us not sit.'

70. əyni ce-mək-roy

we go-NEG-Let

'Let us not go.'

E. 'Let' with a third person singular positive

It is formed by the prefixation of causative marker **min**- and by the suffixation of command marker –**ro** to verb as exemplified below:

71. əma-ha min-ce-ro

he-ACC CAU-go-COMD.

'Let him go.'

72. əma-ha min-in-ro

he-ACC CAUS-drink-COMD.

'Let him drink.'

F. 'Let' with a third person singular negative

In this formation, the negative marker –**mək** and command marker –**ro** are suffixed to the verb. Then, the causative marker **min-** is prefixed as given below:

73. əma-ha min-ce-mək-ro

he-ACC CAUS-go-NEG-COMD.

'Let him not go.'

74. əma-ha min-in-mək-ro

he-ACC CAUS-drink-NEG-COMD.

'Let him not drink.'

G. 'Let' with a third person plural positive

In Koireng, the command marker –**ru** is suffixed to the verb and the causative marker **min-** is prefixed to the verb to indicate the 'let imperative positive in the case of the third person plural. Examples:

75. ənmani-ha min-ce-ru

they-ACC CAUS-go-COMD.

'Let them go.'

76. ənmani-ha min-in-ru

they-ACC CAUS-drink-COMD.

'Let them drink.'

H. 'Let' with a third person plural negative

It is formed with the negative marker –**mək** and the command marker –**r(u)** which is suffixed to the verb, at the same time the causative marker **min-** is prefixed to the verb as exemplified below:

77. ənma-ni min-ce-mək-ru

they-ACC CAUS-go-NEG-COMD.

'Let them not go.'

78. ənma-ni min-in-mək-ru

they-ACC CAUS-drink-NEG-COMD.

'Let them not drink.'

Peremtory Declarative

In Koireng, peremtory declaratives are also expressed as command. The suffix –**siknini** is used as a peremtory declarative.

Examples;

79. nəŋ iskul ərəptəkkə ce-siknini

you school quickly go-PER.D

'You should go school quickly.'

80. nəŋ ərəptəkkə wa-siknini

you quickly come-PER.D

'You should come quickly.'

10.6 Interrogative

Interrogative features of natural languages can be classified into three groups: Intonation, order and segmental elements; above those, a feature can be added, i.e. interrogative gesture. They are discussed one by one in the followings:

a) Intonation: Which includes sentences and tag intonation as well as particle and interrogative word accent (rising pitch in declarative sentence).

b) Order: Which includes main constituent, inversion, positional relationship of affix to stem and of tag, Question-particle or question-word to clause constituent.

c) Segmental elements: Which include interrogative particle (and affixes), words and tags.

d) Interrogative qesture (eyebrow lifted, head inclined forward etc.).

There are basically two types of interrogatives. One is yes/no question and another is inquiry question, generally known as wh-questions.

Yes/No question

The formation of yes/no question is different from other TB languages, like Manipuri, Thadou, Chothe, Paite etc., in which the question marker is simply suffixed to the verb. In the case of Koireng, the question marker –**mo** is suffixed to the object or subject or numerals: it can also be said that the question marker –**mo** does not add to the verb at all.

Example:

81. nəŋ bu-mo ni-cak
you rice-QUES 2pp.-eat.
'Do you eat rice?'

82. nəŋ iskul-mo ni-ce
you school-QUES 2pp.-go
'Do you go school?'

83. tombə-mo ni-ni
toba-QUES 2pp-be
'(Are you) Tomba?'

84. miriŋ riŋŋa-mo ən-ni
man five-QUES 3pp-be
'Are they five men?'

Wh-Question

In Koireng, wh-question is formed with a question word and a question marker –**mo** or **ye~ke~ŋe~ne~** etc. The question words in this language are **khoy** 'who', **əŋ** 'what', **əŋcat** 'which', **əŋsika/ əŋyara** 'why', **ətik** 'when', **honə/hunə**'where', **əŋŋa** 'how' etc.

That question marker –**mo** or or **ye~ke~ŋe~ke~me** etc. can be added to the question word and it gives the meanings as given below:

1. k^hoy-me/k^hoy-mo 'who?' (Who is)
2. əŋ-ŋe/ əŋ-mo 'what?' (What is)
3. əŋcat-te/əŋcat-mo 'which?' (Which is)
4. əŋsik-ke/əŋsik-mo/əŋyara-ye/əŋyara-mo 'why?' (Why is)
5. əŋtikphaa-ye/əŋtikphaa-mo 'when?' (When will)
6. hunə-ye/honə-ye/ hunə-mo/ honə-mo 'where?' (Where is)
7. əŋŋa-ye / əŋa-mo 'how?' (How will)

k^hoy-me/ k^hoy-mo 'who'

In Koireng, **k^hoy** is the wh-question word and **–me/-mo** is the question marker. The question marker –**me/-mo** can suffix to the wh-question word and the verb.

Examples:

85. nəŋ k^hoy-mo   ni-ni

    you   who-QUES   2pp.-be

    'Who are you?'

86. əma-hin k^hoy-koy-mo   ə-ni

    he-NOM   who-call-QUES   3pp-BE

    'Whom does he call?'

əŋ-ŋe/ əŋ-mo 'what'

əŋ- is the wh-question word and –ŋe/-mo is the question marker.

The question marker **–ŋe/-mo** can suffix to the wh-question word and the verb as exemplified below:

87. əŋ-mo

what-QUES

'What (is it)?'

88.

nəŋ	əŋ-cak-mo	ni-ni
you	what-eat-QUES	2pp.-be

'What are you eating?'

əŋca-te/əŋcat-mo 'which'

əŋcat and **–te/-mo** are the wh-qustion word and question marker respectively. The question marker **–mo/-te** can suffix to the wh-question word as given below:

89.

nəŋ	əŋcat-mo	ni-dəy
you	which-QUES	2pp.-like

'Which do you want?'

90.

pon-hi	əŋcat-mo	ə-sa
cloth-DET	which-q.mk.	3pp-beauty

'Which cloth is beauty.'

əŋsik-ke/əŋsik-mo/əmyara-ye/əŋyara-mo 'why?'

əŋsik/əŋyara is the qh-question word and **–ke/-ye/-mo** is the question marker. The question marker **–ke/-ye/-mo** can be suffixed to wh-question word and the verb.

Examples:

91.

nəŋ	əŋsik-mo	ni-ce
you	why-QUES	2pp.-go

'Why are you going?'

92. əŋsik nay cəp-mo ə-ni

why child cry-QUES 3pp.-BE

'Why is the baby crying?'

əŋtikpʰaa-ye/əŋtikpʰaa-mo 'when?'

əŋtikpʰaa is the wh-question word and **–ye/-mo** is the question marker. The question marker can be suffixed to the wh-question word and the verb as exemplified below:

93. nəŋ əŋtikpʰaa-mo ni-kertʰəy

you when-QUES 2pp.-get up

'When do you get up?'

94. nəŋ əŋtikpʰaa-om-mo ni-ni

you when-born-QUES 2pp-BE

'When are you born?'

honə-ye/honə-ye/ hunə-mo/ hunə-mo 'where?'

hunə/honə is the wh-question word and **–ye/-mo** is the question marker. The question marker can be suffixed to the wh-question word as exemplified below:

95. hunə-mo

where-QUES

'Where (are going)?'

96. əma hunə-mo ə-ce

he where-QUES 3pp-go

'Where does he go?'

əŋŋa-ye / əŋŋa-mo 'how?'

In Koireng, **əŋŋa** is the wh-question word and **–ye/-mo** is the question marker. The question marker **–mo/-ye** can be suffixed to the wh-question word.

Examples:

97. əma kerloy-ha əŋŋa-mo ə-ni
he slip-DET how-q.mk 3pp-BE
'How does he slip?'

98. əma-hin əŋŋa-mo pəysa ə-pek
he-nom. how-QUES.money 3pp.-give
'How does he gives money?'

Alternative Question

In Koireng, alternative questions are formed by adding the question marker –**mo** to the both alternative of nouns and pronouns or adverbs. In the case of verb it does not arise. In the formation of alternative questions **əniməkle** 'or is used as coordinator. They are discussed below:

Alternative of Noun

99. hina waha dimhomo əni əniməkle coŋtemo ə-ni
here come-DET dimho-QUES 3pp-BE or Chongte-QUES 3pp.-be
'Does Dimho or Chongte come here?'

100. nəŋ ni-dəy-ha pon-mo ni-ni əniməkle soŋkol-mo ni-ni
you like-DET cloth-QUES 2pp-BE or shirt-q.mk. 2pp-be
'Do you like cloth or shirt?'

Alternative of Verbs

101. nəŋ kop^{h}i-mo ni-ni əniməkle in-ləy-mo ni-ni
you coffee-QUES 2pp.-drink or drink-NEG-QUES 2pp-BE
'Do you drink coffee or not?'

102. nəŋ iskul-mo ni-ce əniməkle ce-ləy-mo ni-ni
you school-QUES 2pp.-go or go-NEG-QUES 2pp-BE
'Do you go to school or not?'

Alternative of Adverbs

103. əma yoŋ-ha ərəppə-mo ə–ni ənimәkle əcummə-mo ə-ni

he come-DET quickly-QUES.3pp-be or slowly-QUES.3pp-BE

'Does he come quickly or slowly?'

104. nəŋ bu cak-ha ətəmmə-mo ni-ni ənimәkle ətommə-mo ni-ni

you rice eat-DET very-QUES 2pp-BE or some-QUES 2pp-BE

'Do you eat very much or not?'

Tag Question

In Koireng, tag question is formed by the suffixation of question marker–**mo** to the verb in the positive tag question while in the negative tag, the negative marker –**mək** is added before the question marker –**mo**. Koireng has reversed tag and constant tag question.

The most commonly indentified function of reversed polarity tag is to obtain 'confirmation', *i.e.* the speaker thinks the proposition is true, but wants the addressec to confirm it. But it is not necessary for the speaker to be uncertain about the truth of the proposition, as this definition impties (otherwise he wouldn't be asking for confirmation of it). The proposition can be analytically true, in which case the speaker must know for certain that is true.

Reversed tag:

105. kʰahoy ə-sa, sa-mək-mo

khahoi 3pp-nice nice-NEG-QUES

'Khahoi is nice, is not she?'

106. əma yu ə-in, in-məkmo

he liquor 3pp-drink drink-NEG.QUES

'He drinkds liquor, doesn't he?'

107. hiwahi tuy-mək-e, ə-tuy-mo

it tasty-NEG-NCP 3pp-tasty-QUES

'It is not tasty, is it?'

108. əma ə-hoŋ, hoŋ-mək-mo

he 3pp.-come come-NEG-QUES

'He comes, doesn't he?'

It is already known that the speaker wants confirmation of this proposition that 'Khahoi is nice' as given in sentence (105) so he added tag part. It is also known in the used as in sentence (105), (106) and (108) while in the positive tag question the pronominal prefix is used as in **ə-** 3rd person pronominal prefix is used (**ə-tuy-mo**). From the previous sentences, we can see how the tag-question is formed:

a)

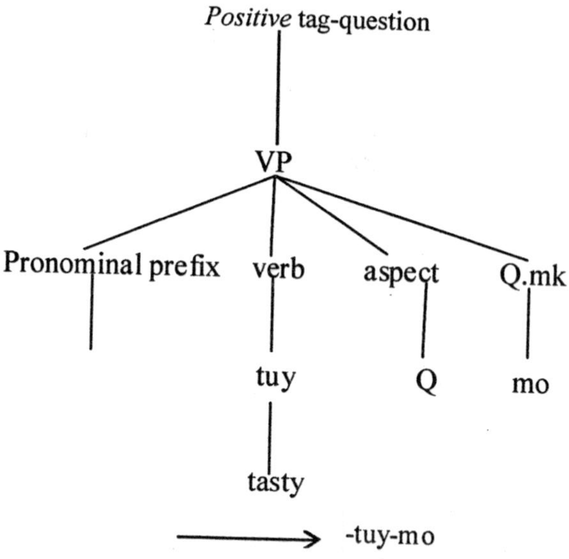

b) Negative tag-question

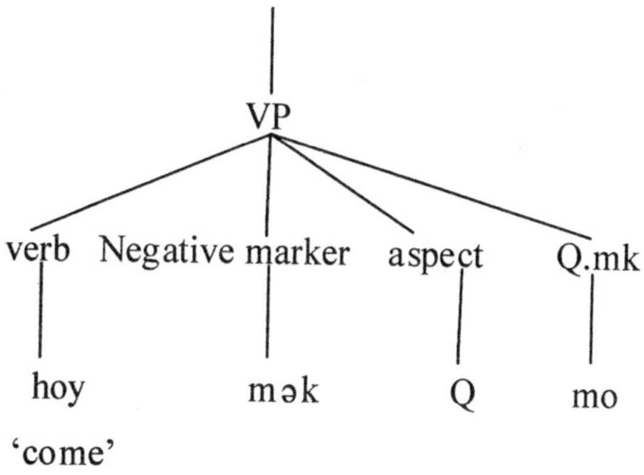

→ hoy-mək-mo

Constant Tag

109. k^hahoy ə-sa-mo

khahoy 3pp-nice-QUES

'Khahoi is nice, is she?'

110. əma-han soŋkol k^hət ə-hoŋcoy, ə-hoŋcoy-mo

he-nom. shirt one 3pp-bring 3pp-bring-QUES

'He brings a shirt, does he?'

111. əma yu in-mək-e, in-mək-mo

he liquor drink-NEG-NCP drink-NEG.QUES

'He doesn't drink liquor, doesn't he?'

Tag question in Imperative

Tag question also can be attached not only to declarations, but also to imperative sentences. In this also reversed tag as well as constrant tag are used.

112. cuon-ha t^{h}o-ro, cuon-mo t^{h}o-ni-te

work-DET do-COMD work-QUES do-2pp-UNRE

'Do the work, will you?'

113. curup yop-mək-ro, curup-moypo-ni-te

cigaratte drink-NEG-COMD. cigaratte-q.mk. drink-2pp-UNRE

'Don't smoke, will you?'

114. cuon-ha t^{h}o-ro, cuon-mo t^{h}o-mək-ni-te

work-DET do-COMD. work-QUES do-NEG-2pp-UNRE

'Do the work, won't you?'

The formation of tag part (in inperative sentence) is different from tag in declarative sentences. That is, here, the whole sentence is repeated but the command marker is not used, as in the above sentence. Semantically there is no intention on the part of the speaker 'to obtain confirmation' nor 'to express shared beliefs but only to make it imperative with a definite sense (*i.e.* to make the addnessce understand that it should be done without fail).

10.7 Optative Sentence

It expresses wishes and it is formed through the suffixation – **rise** to the verb.

Examples:

115. əma-ha pət^{h}iennin sən-rise

he-DET good save-WISH

'God may save him'

116. əma riŋso-rise

he long live-WISH

'May he live long.'

117. əma-ha hoy-rise

he-DET happy-WISH

'May he live happily.'

10.8 Exclamatory Sentence

Exclaimatory expresses the sudden feelings and emotion of happiness and sorrow. The word **o^h orəŋkuimәna** expresses the sudden emotion of sorrow and the word **sawat/ tut/ təg/əs** expresses the sudden emotion of happiness as exemplified below:

118. oh! əma ca-ha ə-t^{h}ie

Alas he son-DET 3pp-die.

'Alas! His son is dead!'

119. sawat əyni-hin ni-tor-yəy

match we-NOM 1pp-win-PERF

'We have won the match.'

120. əs əŋŋa-sa la-mo -ni

surprise how-nice song-QUES 3pp-BE

'How nice is the song!'

11

Reduplication

11.1 Reduplication

Reduplication is that repetition, the result of which constituteted the unit word. Reduplication can be classified into four, namely complete, partial, echo and mimic. Complete reduplete, according to Apte (1968) is of three main types: (i) repetition of a one-word utterance, (ii) repetition of a clause or phrase and (iii) repetition of single morpheme and/or words. Reduplication is a linguistic feature analysed in 'India as a linguistic area' by Masica (1976). Tibeto-Burman languages, namely, Burmese, Lahu, Manipuri etc are rich in reduplication.

Koireng is also rich in complete reduplication and is used very commonly in speech. Complete reduplication is found in nouns, Wh-questions, adjectives, adverbs, verbs; (repletion of verb is generally found in command, request and informative statements.

Reduplication, generally, has many different semantic shades in a language: reduplication has the meanings of distributiveness, plurality, emphatic and endearing attitude. Koireng has also the above meaning.

In Koireng, reduplication can occur in nouns, wh-question words, adjectives, adverbs and verbs. They are given below:

Noun

Examples;

in	'house'	inin	'respective houses/houses'
ka	'room'	kaka	'respective rooms/rooms'
k^{h}ət	'one'	k^{h}ət k^{h}ət	'one each'

They occur in sentences.

1. naypəŋ əcəŋ in in rikip^{h}a ən-ce

   children all house house every 3pp.-go

   'All the children go to every house.'

2. laŋmayciŋ/soŋni-ə ka ka rikip^{h}a t^{h}eṛ-ro

   Sunday-LOC room room every clean-COMD.S

   'Clean all rooms on the Sunday.'

3. mit^{h}ay k^{h}ət k^{h}ət pe-ro

   sweets one one give-COMD.---------

   'Give the sweets to one each.'

Wh-questions

In Koireng, repetition of wh-question words are used very frequently. Examples are given below:

k^{h}oy-k^{h}oy-mo

who-who-QUES

'Who who'

əŋ-əŋ-mo

what-what-QUES

'What what'

hunə-hunə-mo

where-where-QUES

'Where where'

They can be seen occurring in the following sentences.

4. k^{h}oy-k^{h}oy-mo iskul ən-ce

who-who-QUES school 3pp-go

'Who(pl.) are going to school?'

5. nəŋ əŋ-əŋ-mo ni-cak

you what-what-QUES 2pp-eat

What (pl.) are you eating?'

6. nəŋ əŋcat-əŋcat-mo ni-dəy

you which-which-QUES 2pp.-like

'Which(pl.) do (you) want?'

Adjectives

Examples:

əsen	'red'	əsen əsen	'red red'
əbəŋ	'white'	əbəŋ əbəŋ	'white white'
əsaŋ	'tall'	əsaŋ əsaŋ	'tall tall'

They occur in the following sentences:

7. əma-han ṛəypar əsen əsen əcəŋ ə-k^{h}iyek

she-NOM flower red red all 3pp.-pluck

'She plucks all red (red) flowers.'

8. əma-han soŋkol əbəŋ əbəŋ əcəm ə-ricok

she-nom. shirt white white all 3pp-buy

'She buys all white (white) shirts.'

9. əmanin t^hiŋ əsaŋ əsaŋ ə-tuk
   they tree tall tall 3pp.-cut
   'They cut all the tall (tall) trees.'

Adverbs

Examples:

yam-mə	'slow'	yamyam-mə	'slowly and slowly'
nuy-yə	'smile'	nuynuy-yə	'smile and smile'
ərəp-pə	'fast'	ərəp-pə	'fast and fast'

They can be seen from the following examples;

10. əma yam yam-mə ə-ce
    he slow slow-ADV 3pp-go
    'He goes slowly, slowly.'

11. əma nuy nuy-yə ə-ce
    he smile smile-ADV 3pp-go
    'He goes by smiling.'

12. kəyni nisowo yiŋtiyeŋ ərəp ərp-pə kin-ce
    we generally walk fast fast-ADV 3pp-go
    'We generally walk fast (fast) in the morning.'

Verbs

In the case of verbs, it differs from other reduplication of nouns, wh-question words, adverbs and adjectives. Reduplication of verb (in certain context) becomes a sentence, and named as sentential reduplication. This is grammatically possible in different types of sentence construction, such as, informative statement, command and request. They are discussed below:

Informative statement

In this case, the speaker is informing the addressee, occurring just at the moment of departure as in the following sentences.

13. ki-le-ce ki-le-ce

 1pp-PROG 1pp-PROG

 'I am going.'

14. ki-le-t^həw ki-le-t^həw

 1pp-PROG-do 1pp-PROG-do

 'I am doing.'

II COMMAND

The subject is definitely second person though it is not overtly in the structure and repetition of such type is very commonly used in speech. This is a subject-object-less structure. Command is formed by the suffixation to the action oriented verbal root as exemplified below:

15. ce-ro ce-ro

 go-COMD. go-COMD.

 '(You) go.'

16. in-ro in-ro

 drink-COMD. drink-COMD.

 '(You) drink.'

III REQUEST

Reduplication of verb is also used in request also, for instance;

17. ni-in-pek-ro

 2pp-drink-HON-COMD.S

 'Please drink.'

18. ni-ce-pek-ro

    2pp-go-HON-COMD.S

    'Please go.'

12

Social Grammar

12.1 Forms of Address

Forms of address in a society are closely related to social structure as well as inter personal relationship between the addressee and speaker. Forms of address are conditioned by kinship relation or age or the ego–male or female.

1. Kinship terms of address

In Koireng, the term of address are closely related to kinship terms. The kinship terms are used for different kinship relationship as exemplified below:

1.	kipa	'my father'
2.	kinu	'my mother'
3.	kitərpi	'mother-in-law'
4.	kitərpu	'father-in-law'
5.	kinulien	'mother's sister (elder)'
6.	kipalien	'father's brother (elder)'
7.	kiunu	'sister (elder)'
8.	kinəynu	'sister (younger)'

9.	kinute	'cousin(sister)'
10.	kipate	'cousin(brother)'
11.	kinote	'aunt'
12.	kipu	'brother-in-law'
13.	kiunu	'sister-in-law'
14.	kine	'father's sister'

The first syllable **ki** is derived from kəy 'I' and **ki** is a also a first person pronominal marker which is prefixed in all the kinship terms. All these kinship terms are used by irrespective of the male and female egos.

2. Address by Name

In Koireng, the most common form of address is to call a person by his or her name. If a person's name is **'Somel'** the elders of his family address him by his name Somel.

The wife does not call her husband by name instead of it, the word **əpa** 'his father is used. A husband calls to his wife **ənu** 'his mother or by 'name.'

3. Age Difference

Age is also an important deciding factor for terms of address in Koireng society among the non–kins and among the kins of same generation. The kinship terms are extended to address and choose the appropriate terms.

Age Group	*Address term*	
Fatherly old	kipalien	'father's brother (elder)
Fatherly old	kipate/pasien 'uncle'	
Fatherly old	kipu	'mother's brother'
brotherly old	kiupa	'elder brother'
sisterly old	kiunu	'elder sister'

motherly old	kinu	'mother'
motherly old	kine	'father's sister'

12.2 Naming System

Koireng has culture of naming their son or daughter according to order. The first son is named as **upa / cəpa** and the first daughter is named as **cənuupa**. The second son or daughter is named as **milay**. The last son and daughter are named as **cəlutir** and **mitun** respectively.

12.1.3 Taboo

Linguistic taboo or the fact of avoiding mentioning certain words, phrases and expressions in a language is a common practice in a society. It is conventionally prohibited words or expressions to mention in certain times or else. It is a matter of convention where the normal use of an item in a language is inhibited due to a particular social values and beliefs (Trudgill, 1986:29). The taboo words reflect the values and beliefs of a society. They an determined by some factors like religion, belief, social condition and psychology of the people. The taboo items vary from one society to another. According to Trudgill (ibid:30), the strongest taboo words in a the English-speaking world are still associated with sex, followed by those associated with exerction. In Norway, they are mostly expressions connected with the devil, and in Roman catholic culture, they are words essentially associated with religion. The taboo words of Koireng are associated with sex, personal names, k in terms, animals names etc: they are categorized in the following ways:

(i) Taboo on personal names

(ii) Taboo in kin terms

(iii) Taboo on some animal names

(iv) Taboo on the use of certain words at night

(v) Taboo words associated with sex etc.

I. Taboo of personal name

As a taboo a wife does not call her husband's name but calls him by some teknonyms. She may address her husband by taking her eldest son's or daughter's name or elder brother, for example, **əpa** 'his father.' **kiupa/upa** 'elder brother' etc.

In Koireng custom, it is not permitted to address older people by their personal names. The kinship addressing terms are extended and used the appropriate one, as given in the following:-

Male	*Female*
kiupa 'elder brother'	kiunu 'elder sister'
kipa 'daddy'	kinu 'mother'
pate 'uncle'	nute 'aunty'
kipu 'mother's brother'	kine 'mother's brother wife'

II. Taboo in kin Terms

In Koireng, there is a very strict rule to avoid relationship between elder brother-in-law and younger-sister-in-law: it is to some extent not permitted to talk closely in proximity and directly. The elder brother-in-law can call her by name but the younger sister-in-law cannot call him by name. She used the term **kiupa** or **əupa** 'elder brother'.

III. Taboo on Some Animal Names

The name of some dangerous animals like **humpi** 'tiger' **rul** 'snake' etc. are forbidden to be mentioned specially in the forest. In lieu of these names displaced words such as **rutnu** 'dangerous animal' and (for **humpi** 'tiger') **ruyyam** 'climber' (for **rul** 'snake')are used respectively.

IV. Taboo on the use of certian words at Night

In Koireng, it is not allowed to utter and use the word **simphoy** 'needle' at night. The word **o** 'yes' is taboo word. Instead of saying **o** 'yes' is advised to say **əŋsikiəni** 'why are you calling'.

V. Taboo words associated with Sex

Words which are associated with sex and their functions are

prohibited to be used in public places. Generally people consider use of such words obscene and bad manner. Euphemistic words are used e.g. **naymince** 'to throw child' for **nayhe** 'abortion', **nayom** 'to have child' for **naynəy** 'to give birth' **əray** 'conceived' for **nayron** 'pregnant' etc.

Vocabulary

Eglish to Koireng Vocabulary

Able	ətoṛ/əyəy
Absent	əliepjok
Admit	əlut
Advance	məsək
After	nukka
Again	t^{h}əwk^{h}ir
Age	kum
Agree	nom
Aid	sənna
Air	p^{h}əywo
Air	t^{h}iraŋ/p^{h}ywo
All	ərek^{h}uwa
Almirah	upu
Alone	ət^{h}yya
Also	num
Always	ərikkippə
And	həko/hənnako

Anger luŋt^{h}ək

Animal sa

Animal yulewa

Annex minkeṛcun

Answer keṛdəŋ

Antonym miletmik^{h}up

Appetite woncam

Apple t^{h}əyt^{h}up

Appoint cuonpek

April mertun

Arm ban

Around ərəmlikkipə

Arrive watuŋ

Arrow t^{h}əl

Ash wut

Ask ṛilkel

August jiŋpi

Aunt kinote

Axe ṛəy

Baby naypəŋ

Bachelor rolt^{h}əṛ/rot^{h}ər

Back nuk

Back-bone ṛoŋru

Bad yalk^{h}um

Bake	hay
Ball	bol
Bamboo	ro
Ban	k^{h}ar
Banana	mot
Bank	ək^{h}əm
Barber	səmepmi
Bark	t^{h}iŋkoṛ
Basket	bor/p^{h}ur
Bat	bak
Bath	tuybol
Beak	waneṛ
Bean	be
Bean	be
Bear	səwəm
Bear	ra
Beat	wok
Beauty	sət
Bed	yalk^{h}um
Bed sheet	kicəw
Bee	k^{h}oi
Beef	seratmesa
Before	mateŋ
Begin	p^{h}utna

Bell	kaŋsi
Belly	won
Below	ənoyya
Berry	biet
Between	əkarra
Big	lien
Bind	$ək^hir$
Bird	wa
Bird	wa
Bitter	$ək^ha$
Black	əwom
Blind	mitcəw
Blind	mitco
Blood	t^hi
Blunt	ŋəyləy
Blur	səŋ
Boat	ṛikuwoŋ
Body	təksa
Body-hair	əmul
Boil	$əbut/ə\text{-}p^hul$
Bold	luŋəl
Bone	əyru
Book	larik
Bottle	likli

Bouquet	wuṛkay
Bow	ṛup^{h}el
Bowl	kaŋtṛum
Box	upu
Boy	pasəlte
Bracelet	yaksəṛ
Brain	lut^{h} ok
Brain	lut^{h}ok
Branch	t^{h}iŋcəŋ
Bread	təl/waypol
Break	mik^{h}oy
Breast	rinu
Breathe	p^{h}ukləy
Breeze	p^{h}əyworaŋhiyəy
Brick	cek
Bridge	t^{h}oŋ
Bright	əde
Bring	həycoy
Brinjal	pənco
Brother (e)	kiupa
Brother (y)	kinaypa
Brother	ulənay
Brother's wife (e)	əkiunu
Brother's wife (y)	cainanəw

Bubble	əp^{h}on
Bud	ədon
Buffalo	seləwwe
Bug	keṛcat
Bull	seratcəl
Bull	selatcəl
Bunch	əbom
Burn	əkaŋ
Busy	toŋləy
Butter	serinutuytt^{h}ay
Butterfly	pelep
Cabbage	kobi
Cabbage	kopi
Cage	teŋwoŋ
Calculate	thəw
Calf	sete
Calm	nulcənday
Camel	səŋoŋsəy/səriŋsəy
Cane	tiŋ
Care	keṛret
Carry	ən
Cat	ŋaytoŋ/meŋte
Catch	cur
Cattle	insa

Cauliflower	kopit^{h}əcet
Chair	cokki
Chalk	kakru
Change	ət^{h}ur
Chapter	ərup
Charm	p^{h}ilt^{h}ət
Chase	cuṛ
Cheap	ənem
Cheat	lemlet
Cheek	əŋiem
Cheese	serinutuyp^{h}ən
Chest	ərop
Chicken	arne
Chicken	ar
Child	nayte
Child	nay
Children	naypəŋ
Chilli	miṛca
Chin	ək^{h}a
Choice	dəyt^{h}əŋ
Claw	kuttin
Clay	beheṛ
Clear	ət^{h}eŋ
Climb	əkəl

Close	ək^{h}aṛ
Cloth	pon
Cloud	sump^{h}ay
Coal	məyhol
Coat	kot
Cock	arkhoŋ
Cockroach	k^{h}aŋlay
Coconut	yupi
Coin	pəysa/dəŋka
Cold	əday
Collect	risay
Collide	keṛt^{h}eŋ
Colour	əṛie
Colour	əroŋ/ərie
Combine	minkeṛcun
Come	wa
Commence	əhoŋsok
Common cold	k^{h}əwbuṛ
Compose	minkercun
Condition	əomcən
Consider	keṛk^{h}əlna
Console	mit^{h}em
Conspire	keṛṛolda
Continue	əban

Cook	suoŋ
Cooked rice	bu
Cottage	inte
Cotton	pəttəm
Country	ṛəm
Courage	əṛat
Court-yard	toltaŋ
Cousin (brother)	kipate
Cousin (sister)	kinute
Cow	seratpi
Coward	paŋləy/əsuol
Cow-dung	seek
Cow-shed	serikul/sekuol
Cradle	kaykolen
Crane	oynu
Crow	waak
Crude	əcok
Cuckoo	tiktiniŋ
Cucumber	cəkma
Current	tuytan
Curry	ən
Cut	ətən
Daddy (father)	kipa
Dagger	cemyam

Damage	əməŋ
Dance	lam
Danger	t^{h}inərəp
Dark	əjiŋ
Date-palm	kino
Day	ənik^{h}uwor
Day after tomorrow	nəktip
Day before yesterday	nik^{h}ətni
Deaf	korset
Deaf	koṛset
Dear	niŋsiet
Debt	pəysarat
Decade	nəynakyoŋkoy
December	birip
Decide	keṛp^{h}ut
Deer	sək$_{h}$i
Define	mint^{h}əyt^{h}eŋ
Delay	nukcum
Demand	ləyroŋ
Den	ṛəmsulkar
Depend	kiby
Derive	sinsət
Desert	ləyŋoyṛəm
Destroy	minməŋhot

Devil	b^{h}ut
Dew	ṛoday
Diarrhoea	eksen
Die	ət^{h}ir
Difficult	əlutək/ək^{h}oktək
Dig	əcəy
Dirty	əcok
Disease	nutsietwoy
Distance	əlak
Divide	keṛsem
Divorce	keṛsen
Do	əsin/ət^{h}o
Dog	uy
Donkey	sekel
Door	ink^{h}aṛ
Door	ink^{h}aṛ
Dragonfly	wuysteŋdot
Dream	ruməŋ
Dress	keṛrit^{h}okna
Drink	in
Drive	əmisiet
Dry	əhay
Duck	artok
Dumb	coŋboy

Dust	utp^{h}u
Duty	con
Each	k^{h}ətk^{h}ətta
Eagle	laŋkiya
Ear	koṛ
Earth	ləypil
Earth	wanoyləysiet
East	nisokteŋ
Eat	cak
Egg	aṛtuy
Eight	kiriet
Eight hundred	riyariet
Eight thousand	lisiŋriet
Eighteen	somləytiet
Eighth	kirietsunna
Eighty	somriet
Eighty eight	somrietləyriet
Eighty five	somrietləyriŋŋa
Eighty four	somrietləyli
Eighty nine	somrietləyko
Eighty one	somrietləyk^{h}ət
Eighty seven	somrietləysəri
Eighty six	somrietləyruk
Eighty three	somrietləyt^{h}um

Eighty two	somrietləyni
Elbow	kutki
Elder	kiu
Elephant	saypi
Eleven	somk^{h}ət
Empty	əruok
End	ətoṛəcay
Enemy	melma
Enter	luk
Equal	keṛəŋ
Escape	əkellip
Evening	nitatteŋ
Event	rəysuuop
Evil	sələy
Express	ṛilsuop
Eye	mit
Eye-brow	mitmul
Eye-lash	mitboṛ
Face	may
Fail	duktoŋ
Fall	əyoŋta
Famine	bulut
Fat	əməṛ
Father's brother (e)	kipalien
Father's sister	kine

Father-in-law	ki-təroy
Fathers brother (y)	kipasien
Fear	citrat
February	wulpi
Feet	ke
Fever	ritun
Fifteen	somləyriŋŋa
Fifth	riŋŋasunna
Fifty	somriŋŋa
Fifty eight	somriŋŋaləyriet
Fifty five	somriŋŋaləyriŋŋa
Fifty four	somriŋŋaləyli
Fifty nine	somriŋŋaləykc
Fifty one	somriŋŋaləyk^{h}ət
Fifty seven	somriŋŋaləysəri
Fifty six	somriŋŋaləyruk
Fifty three	somriŋŋaləyt^{h}um
Fifty two	somriŋŋaləyni
Find	əban
Fire	məy
Fire-wood	t^{h}iŋ
First	əcumtək
Fish	ŋa
Five	riŋŋa

Five hundred	riyariŋŋa
Five thousand	lisiŋriŋŋa
Flame	myri
Flat	əpak
Flesh	əwoy
Float	ətonlan
Floor	ləymay
Fly	mit^{h}əy
Fly(v)	ə.yoŋ
Fog	waŋwoy
Fold	haŋ/t^{h}ep
Food	caklenek
Fool	pəŋ
Forehead	cəl
Forget	minil
Fort	ralpəl
Forty	somminli
Forty eight	somminliləyriet
Forty five	somminliləyriŋŋa
Forty four	somminliləyli
Forty nine	somminliləykɵ
Forty one	somminliləyk^{h}ət
Forty seven	somminliləysəri
Forty six	somminliləyruk

Forty three	somminliləyt^{h}um
Forty two	somminliləyni
Four	minli
Four hundred	riyaminli
Four thousand	lisiŋminli
Fourteen	somləyli
Fourth	minlisunna
Fox	ṛəmuy
Fresh	ləy$_{h}$ariŋ
Friday	k^{h}oŋluŋni
Friend	ṛuolkeṛlop
Frog	gaw
Fruit	t^{h}əy
Frying pan	k^{h}ay
Full-moon	t^{h}aṛilni
Fun	coŋciem
Future	nopkasik
Game	kerkay
Garden	ṛəykol
Garden lizard	kəykiyin
Garlic	k^{h}ason
Gate	pəl
Gentle	keṛtocənp^{h}ut
Get	ban

Ginger	ayt^{h}iyiŋ
Ginger	kutməl
Girl	numəyte
Girl	numəyte
Give	pek
Glad	niŋsət
Glass	misiel
Go	ce
Goat	kel
God	pat^{h}ien
Gold	sona
Good	sa/st
Goose	kaŋŋa
Gourd	umt^{h}um
Grapes	t^{h}əybom
Grass	səcak
Grass-hopper	k^{h}ay
Grave	t^{h}an
Great	niraŋniləl
Green	əem
Green chilly	mrcariŋ
Group	ri$_h$oy
Guava	puŋəyton
Gum	haṛuy

Gun	selay
Habit	əomcən
Hair	səm
Half	heṛk^{h}ət
Hand	kut
Handicap	namək^{h}ətwat
Hang	k^{h}itk^{h}ay
Hard	ŋəṛ
Harm	məŋ
Hate	nikiṛ
Hawk	k^{h}unuk^{h}ərəŋ
He	əma
Head	lu
Headache	lunut
Hear	ŋay
Heart	luŋ
Hearth	əluŋ
Heat	lum
Heavy	rik
Heel	kedil
Hen	arpi
Her	əmta
Here	hin
Hide	t^{h}ap

Hill	ciŋ
Him	əmayeŋ
Hip	moŋ/toṛ
His	əmta
Hit	wokkicon
Hole	ək^{h}uṛ
Honest	wont^{h}eŋ
Honey bee	k^{h}oi
Hope	taksəŋ
Horn	riki
Horse	sek^{h}or
Hour	puŋ
House	in
How	əŋŋaye/əŋŋamo
Humble	əwonlien
Hurt	keṛseso
I	kəy
Ice	wuṛ
Ideal	yomsət
Idle	t^{h}asiet
Ill	na
Image	lilin
In	əsuŋ
Incline	əkay

Increase	ək^{h}er
Index/Iron finger	kutcəl
Indigestion	wonpor
Infinite	ətoṛtukomləy
Ink	muk
Ink-pot	mukp^{h}u
Inquire	ril
Insects	luŋp^{h}ur
Insult	yək
Intestine	ril
Invent	kəysok
Iron	t^{h}ir
Island	it^{h}ət
It	hiwa$_h$i
Itching	ət^{h}ək
Jack-fruit	jamp^{h}oŋ
January	towulbuwol
jar	bel
Jealous	ersək
Joints	lillo
Journey	walolna
Joy	ə$_h$oy/əhay
Juice	t^{h}əytuy
July	t^{h}əmuṛ

Jump	kicoŋop
June	əypa
Jute	limol
Keep	tet
Key	so
Kick	peṛ
Kill	t^{h}ət
King	reŋ
King fisher	wakkəykoŋ
Kiss	jop
Kitchen	inkil
Kite	teləŋga
Knife	cemte
Know	t^{h}əy
Knowledge	luŋci
Ladder	kəldak
Ladies finger	beləndri
Lame	kekiet
Lantern	ləttelməysər
Lap	dəŋk^{h}o
Large	lien
Last	toṛna
Last	ətərna/ əcayna
Late	k^{h}oboy

Laugh	nuy
Leaf	əbu
Leak	əbeŋ/əweŋ
Learn	keṛcu
Leech	tilpat
Left	woy
Lemon	cəmpra
Length	səy
Lick	əlek
Life	ṛik^ho
Light	ə-waṛ
Like	dəy
Lily	t^həro
Line	əjek
Lion	k^holsa
Lip(s)	neṛ
Liquid	ətuy
Liquor	yu
Liquor	yu
Little finger	kuttenieŋ
Liver	ət^hin
Local physician	t^hiempu
Lock	wayk^hu
Look	en

English	Koireng
Looking glass	meŋsel
Loose	keṛt^{h}ol
Love	niŋsiet
Low	ənem
Lungs	cop
Made	əsin
Magnet	t^{h}iṛjop
Man	pasəl
Man	pasəl
Mango	t^{h}əyhay
March	caypi
Market	kəyt^{h}iel
Marriage	moyroy
Mat	p^{h}eṛ
Mat	p^{h}eṛ
Match	sawat
	əŋsikke/əŋsikmo
Mattress	monpak
Mattress	molpak
May	p^{h}urpa
Me	kəynu
Meal	cənnəp^{h}a
Meat	me
Medicine	ləyliay

Medicine	ləyliay
Meet	keṛmu
Melt	əhoŋp^{h}ulyoṛ
Mid-day	suəncim
Middle finger	kutlayta
Mid-night	yaəncim
Midwife	naycənəy
Milk	serinutuy
Modest	day
Mole	saldum
Monday	yəyni
Monkey	joŋ
Month	t^{h}a
Moon	t^{h}a
Moon	t^{h}a
Morning	jiyiŋteŋ
Morning	yikeŋ
Morsel	bubeŋ
Mosquito	saŋsan
Mosquito-net	kaŋkəl
Mother	ənu
Mother	kinu
Mother's brother	kipu
Mother's sister (e)	kinulien

Mother's sister (y)	kinute
Mother-in-law	kitəṛpi
Mourn	caluŋləy
Moustache	k^hamul
Mouth	neṛ
Mud	del
Multiply	puribə
Mustard	əncəm
Mustard oil	əncəmriek
My	kəyta
Nail	kultin
Name	miŋ
Naval	lay
Neck	əṛiŋ
Nerve	rit^haruy
Nest	waribu
Net	caŋ
New	$ət^h$əṛ
New year	$kumt^h$ər.
New-moon	t^hat^hi
News	$coŋt^h$əŋ
Next	əban
Next	əban
Nice	əsa

Night	yan
Nightingale	k^{h}aykolilok
Nine	ko
Nine hundred	riyako
Nine thousand	lisiŋko
Nineteen	somləyko
Ninety	somko
Ninety eight	somkoləyriet
Ninety five	somkoləyriŋŋa
Ninety four	somkoləyli
Ninety nine	somkoləyko
Ninety one	somkoləyk^{h}ət
Ninety seven	somkoləysəri
Ninety six	somkoləyruk
Ninety three	somkoləyt^{h}um
Ninety two	somkoləyni
Ninth	kosunna
Noise	curti
North	sinteŋ
Nose	narṛ
November	t^{h}əp^{h}əl
Now	ətun
Oath	k^{h}omakkersam
Ocean	tuylayluŋ

Ocean	tuyt^{h}əmpi
October	eṛt^{h}a
Old	upa
On	əcuŋ
One	kink^{h}ət
One hundred	riyak^{h}ət
One thousand	lisiŋk^{h}ət
Onion	tilləw
Open	əloŋ
Oppose	keṛeŋpi
Orange	kommila
Origin	hoŋkeṛt^{h}okna
Ornament	lilieŋ
Other	ək^{h}ətna
Our	əyninu
Owl	simbu
Paddy	ca
Page	pil
Pair	bopk^{h}ət
Palace	konuŋ
Palm	kutp^{h}a
Papaya	t^{h}iŋcəkma
Paper	ce
Paper	ce

Parrot	kirki
Patient	ənə
Pea	məŋkəl
Peacock	wakuwoŋ
Pear	naspati
Pen	kolom
pencil	pencil
Pepper	mərca
Picture	lilim
Piece	əheṛ
Pig	wok
Pigeon	wasu
Pillow	luk^{h}əm
Place	əmuŋ
Plate	k^{h}eŋ
Play	keṛday
Plum	t^{h}əyk^{h}a
Pomegranate	kəpot^{h}əy
Pond	puk^{h}ri
Poor	əreŋ
Pork	wokme
Pot	k^{h}eŋ
Potato	alu
Pour	əbun

Praise	əpak
Prepare	əkeṛriŋ
Prize	mana
Property	ələl
Prose	rilkumpu
Proud	keṛminlen/əor
Pull	əkəy
Pumpkin	may
Puppy	uyte
Pure	$ət^{h}$eŋtək
Put	ədiek
Quality	ɔciŋəwar
Quality	əmətiḳcən
Quarrel	keṛŋəw
Quench	nəmcənna
Quilt	ponsil
Quilt	$kant^{h}$ə
Quite	nipuytuk
Race	tankersiet
Rain	ro
Rainy season	$curt^{h}$a
Rat	miju
Read	pa
Reap	peṛ

Record	ək^{h}um
Red	əsen
Reduce	wat
Reed	t^{h}iŋkaŋ
Rent	əmən
Repeat	ləyk^{h}ət
Rest	col
Result	ət^{h}əŋ
Return	wəkir
Revise	əenno
Rice	bu
Rice	cəcay
Riddle	ken$_{h}$uoŋ
Ride	miciet
Right	cəŋ
Ring	kutki
Ripe	əmin
Rise	keṛt^{h}y
River	tuyduŋ
River	tuywaduŋ
Road	ləmpi
Road	ləmpi
Rock	keṛnok
Roof	incuŋ

English	Koireng
Roof	incuŋ
Room	ka
Room	ka
Root	riyuŋ
Rope	ruy
Rotten	ət^{h}u
Round	kehil
Rub	təkpə
Run	tan
Rush	rəp
Sail	hol
Sale	əyṛo
Saline	micituy
Salt	mici
Salt	mici
Sand	ləyŋoy
Saturday	miremmikənni
Save	kəl
Saw	əmu
Say	ril
Scold	əŋəw
Score	ətəbany
Second	kinnisunna
See	mu

Seed	ru
Seek	kitok
Select	keṛt^həŋ
Send	mince
September	t^harəm
Seven	səri
Seven hundred	riyasəri
Seven thousand	lisiŋsəri
Seventeen	somləysəri
Seventh	sərisunna
Seventy	somsəri
Seventy eight	somsəriləyriet
Seventy five	somsəriləyriŋŋa
Seventy four	somsəriləyli
Seventy nine	somsəriləyko
Seventy one	somsəriləyk^hət
Seventy seven	somsəriləysəri
Seventy six	somsəriləyruk
Seventy three	somsəriləyt^hum
Seventy two	somsəriləyni
Shado	lilim
Shame	əyak
Sharp	ŋəy
She	əma

Sheep	keldoy
Shield	p^{h}əw
Ship	rikoŋ
Shirt	soŋkol
Shirt	soŋkol
Shocks	moja
Shoe	K$_h$oŋup
Shoe	kek^{h}op
Shoot	kap
Shop	tukal
Shop	tukal
Shore	kircorikəl
Shoulder	ədarmek^{h}e
Show	minmu
Shut	k^{h}aṛ
Sing	lat^{h}əw
Sister (e)	kiunulien
Sister (y)	kiunute
Sister-in-law	kiunu
Sit	oŋ
Six	kuruk
Six hundred	riyaruk
Six thousand	lisiŋruk
Sixteen	somləyruk
Sixth	kuruksunna

Sixty	somruk
Sixty eight	somrukləyriet
Sixty five	somrukləyriŋŋa
Sixty four	somrukləyli
Sixty nine	somrukləyko
Sixty one	somrukləyk^{h}ət
Sixty seven	somrukləysəri
Sixty six	somrukləyruk
Sixty three	somrukləyt^{h}um
Sixty two	somrukləyni
Skin	əwun
Sky	wan
Sky	wan
Sky-blue	əpoleŋ
Sleep	in
Sliced bamboo	naŋ
Slow	əcum
Small	sin
Smell	rim
Smile	nuy
Smoke	ək^{h}u
Snail	cokcəl
Snail	cokcəl
Sneeze	kit^{h}em

Snow	uṛ
So	hiŋahi
Soap	sapon
Soil	ləyhaw
Soldier	ṛalmi
Solid	əpəŋ
Some	boṛ/p^{h}uṛ
Song	la
Song	la
Soon	ṛəp
Sorrow	tət
Soul	rit^{h}a
Sound	risa
Soup	ətuy
Source	hoŋsoknəmun
South	maṛtieŋ
Soyabean	beyaŋ
Space	ə$_h$aŋ
Spade	kitu
Sparrow	wacek
Speak	ṛil
Spear	cəy
Spear	cəy
Spend	əlut

Spider	cikməm
Spit	cil
Spoil	əməŋ
Spoon	t^{h}irhayho
Spread	mint^{h}əŋ
Spring	ip^{h}up
Squeeze	əep
Stand	əŋir
Star	əṛsi
Star	aṛsi
Starve	bulut
Steal	rukt^{h}əw
Steam	ərihu
Stem	əkuŋ
Step	kəldakban
Stomach	əp^{h}uŋ
Stone	luŋ
Stop	əŋiṛ
Story	t^{h}urumiŋ
Stream	ṛihu
Strength	ərat
Suck	əjok
Sugar	cini
Sugar	cini

Sugar cane	micu
Sun	ni
Sun	ni
Sunday	soŋni
Surface	nəypillay
Surname	p^huŋ
Sweet potato	kolkay
Swelling	ət^{h}iŋ
Swim	ituywan
Table	tebəl
Taboo	coŋcop
Tail	ruməy
Tailor	ponsuymi
Take	ələy
Tall	saŋ
Tamarind	məŋke
Tame	yək
Tank	puk^{h}ri
Taste	ənik
Tea	ca
Teach	keṛcu
Tea-leaf	cəbuo
Tear	mit^{h}i
Tease	əcok

Teeth	ha
Ten	som
Ten thousand	lisiŋsom
Tenth	somsunna
Test	ədənen
Thatch	nai
Thatch	pət
Their	ənmanita
Them	ənmaninu
There	həwahən
They	ənmani
Thick	əsatul
Thief	meru
Thigh	el
Thin	əkoŋ
Thing	nəynak
Third	kint^{h}umsunna
Thirteen	somləyt^{h}um
Thirty	somt^{h}um
Thirty eight	somt^{h}umləyriet
Thirty five	somt^{h}umləyriŋŋa
Thirty four	somt^{h}umləyli
Thirty nine	somt^{h}umləyko
Thirty one	somt^{h}umləyk^{h}ət

Thirty seven	somtʰumləysəri
Thirty six	somtʰumləyruk
Thirty three	somtʰumləytʰum
Thirty two	somtʰumləyni
Thorn	liŋ
Thought	keṛŋay
Thread	pət
Threat	minci
Three	kinthum
Three hundred	riyathum
Three thousand	lisiŋtʰum
Throat	əṛok
Throw	əwoṛ
Thump	kutpi
Thunder	ṛoṛi
Thursday	uyrəyni
Tie	əkʰit
Tiger	humpi/kamkəy
Time	əpʰa
Tire	yamyəl
Today	wen
Today	wienin
Toe(s)	keməl
Tomato	pəncəwtʰur

Tomorrow	yi-tieŋ
Tongue	ləy
Top	ərol
Touch	tok
Town	k^{h}oppi
Toy	keṛdayna
Trap	caŋ
Travel	lon
Treatment	nutker.en
Tree	t^{h}iŋ
Tremble	kecun
Trouser	k^{h}oŋkraw
True	ət^{h}əy
Try	kellet
Tuesday	telt^{h}uni
Tumbler	um
Twelve	somləyni
Twenty	somni
Twenty eight	somniləyriet
Twenty five	somniləyriŋŋa
Twenty four	somniləyli
Twenty nine	somniləyko
Twenty one	somniləyk^{h}ət
Twenty seven	somniləysəri

Twenty six	somniləyruk
Twenty three	somniləyt^{h}um
Twenty two	somniləyni
Twin	əp^{h}iṛ
Twist	cokk^{h}oy
Two	kinni
Two hundred	riyani
Two thousand	lisiŋni
Ugly	melsiet
Unite	minkeṛcun
Use	ənemna
Vacant	əruop
Vain	ənennaboy
Vast	əlien
Vehicle	kari
Vend	əyoṛ
Very	ətəm
Vibrate	akicuun
Village	khuo
Violet	əpol
Voice	ṛisa
Vomiting	əloksuok
Vulture	milem
Waist	koŋ

Wait	keṛt^{h}əy
Walk	ce
Wall	cekpəl
Wall	sepəl
Wall-lizard	inṛik
Want	dəy
War	ral
Warn	ək^{h}ar
Wash	əṛisuo
Watch	g^{h}ari
Water	tuy
Water	tuy
Wave	ət^{h}ək
Wax	k^{h}ylieŋ
We	əyni
Weak	əsuol
Wealth	ələlət^{h}um
Wedge	ciŋcep
Wednesday	t^{h}əmt^{h}uni
Week	həpta/kark^{h}ət
Week	həpta
Weld	keṛjoṛ
Well	k^{h}uṛ
Well	k^{h}urwadop

West	taytak
West	taytakteŋ
Wet	əcop
What	əŋŋe/əŋmo
Wheat	kehu
When	əŋtikphaaye/əŋtikphaamo
Where	henəye/hunəye
Which	əŋcatte/əŋcatmo
White	əbəŋ
Who	kʰoyme/kʰoymo
Why	əŋyaraye/əŋyaramo
Wicket	sələy
Wide	əpek
Wife	kinuməy
Wild cow	ṛəmsel
Wild duck	ṛəm artok
Wild pig	ṛəmwok
Wild	rəm
Win	ətoṛ
Wind	tʰiraŋ
Window	inkotte
Wing	əmeṛtʰa
Winter	pʰəlbipʰa
Wipe	ənul

Wise	əciŋ
Wish	hoyyəyro
Witch	k^hopu
Woman	numəy
Wood	t^hiŋ
Wool	samul
Wool	samulpuon
Woolen cloths	samulpon
Word	coŋban
Work	cuon
World	noy
Wrist	kutninəy
Write	əjek
Wrong	əlal
Yale	solien
Yawn	əhan
Year	kum
Yeast	əp^{h}on
Yellow	əeŋ
Yes	o
Yesterday	yantieŋ
Yesterday	jannin
Yield	əsok
York	ətoṛna

You	nəŋ
You (pl)	nəŋni
Young	kaŋcotrol
Your	nəŋta
Zero	bindu
Zip	cen
Zodiac	əṛasi
Zone	rəmk^{h}əy
Zoo	sajokin henəmo/hunəmo

Koireng to English Vocabulary

əbəŋ	White
əban	Find
əban	Next
əban	Continue
əbom	Bunch
əbu	Leaf
əbun	Pour
əbut/ə-pʰul	Boil
əbeŋ/əweŋ	Leak
əcəy	Dig
əciŋ	Wise
əciŋəwar	Quality
əcok	Crude
əcok	Dirty
əcok	Tease
əcop	Wet
əcum	Slow
əcumtək	First

əcuŋ	On
ədənen	Test
ədarmek^{h}e	Shoulder
əday	Cold
əde	Bright
ədiek	Put
ədon	Bud
əem	Green
əeŋ	Yellow
əenno	Revise
əep	Squeeze
əhan	Yawn
əhaŋ	Space
əhay	Dry
əheṛ	Piece
əhoŋp^{h}ulyoṛ	Melt
əhoŋsok	Commence
əhoy/əhay	Joy
əjek	Line
əjek	Write
əjiŋ	Dark
əjok	Suck
əkəl	Climb
əkəy	Pull
əkaŋ	Burn

əkarra	Between
əkay	Incline
əkellip	Escape
əkeṛriŋ	Prepare
ək^{h}əm	Bank
ək^{h}ətna	Other
ək^{h}a	Bitter
ək^{h}a	Chin
ək^{h}aṛ	Close
ək^{h}ar	Warn
ək^{h}er	Increase
ək^{h}ir	Bind
ək^{h}it	Tie
ək^{h}u	Smoke
ək^{h}um	Record
ək^{h}uṛ	Hole
əkiunu	Brother's wife (e)
əkoŋ	Thin
əkuŋ	Stem
ələl	Property
ələlət^{h}um	Wealth
ələy	Take
əla	steer
əlak	Distance
əlal	Wrong

əlek	Lick
əlien	Vast
əliepjok	Absent
əloŋ	Open
əloksuok	Vomiting
əluŋ	Hearth
əlut	Admit
əlut	Spend
əlutək/ək^{h}oktək	Difficult
əmən	Rent
əməŋ	Spoil
əməŋ	Damage
əməṛ	Fat
əmeṛt^{h}a	Wing
əmətikcən	Quality
əma	He
əma	She
əmayeŋ	Him
əmin	Ripe
əmisiet	Drive
əmta	Her
əmta	His
əmu	Saw
əmul	Body-hair
əmuŋ	Place

ən	Carry
ən	Curry
əna	Patient
əncəm	Mustard
əncəmriek	Mustard oil
ənem	Low
ənem	Cheap
ənemna	Use
ənennaboy	Vain
əŋəw	Scold
əŋcatte/əŋcatmo	who
əŋiem	Cheek
əŋir	Stand
əŋir	Stop
əŋŋaye/əŋŋamo	How
əŋŋe/əŋmo	What
əŋcatte/əŋcatmo	Which
əŋtikphaaye/əŋtikphaamo	When
əŋyaraye/əŋyaramo	Why
ənik	Taste
ənik^{h}uwor	Day
ənmani	They
ənmaninu	Them
ənmanita	Their
ənoyya	Below

ənu	Mother
ənul	Wipe
əomcən	Condition
əomcən	Habit
əpak	Flat
əpak	Praise
əpek	Wide
$əp^ha$	Time
$əp^hiṛ$	Twin
$əp^hon$	Yeast
$əp^hon$	Bubble
$əp^huŋ$	Stomach
əpol	Violet
əpoleŋ	Sky-blue
ərəmlikkipə	Around
əṛasi	Zodiac
ərat	Strength
əṛat	Courage
$ərek^huwa$	All
əreŋ	Poor
əṛie	Colour
$əri^hu$	Steam
ərikkippə	Always
əṛiŋ	Neck
əṛisuo	Wash

əṛok	Throat
ərol	Top
əroŋ/ərie	Colour
ərop	Chest
əruok	Empty
əruop	Vacant
ərup	Chapter
əṛsi	Star
əsa	Nice
əsatul	Thick
əsen	Red
əsin	Made
əsin/ət^{h}o	Do
əsok	Yield
əsuŋ	In
əsuol	Weak
ətəbany	Score
ətəm	Very
ətən	Cut
ətərna/ əcayna	Last
ət^{h}ək	Wave
ət^{h}ək	Itching
ət^{h}əŋ	Result
ət^{h}əṛ	New
ət^{h}əy	True

ət^{h}eŋ — Clear
ət^{h}eŋtək — Pure
ət^{h}in — Liver
ət^{h}iŋ — Swelling
ət^{h}ir — Die
ət^{h}u — Rotten
ət^{h}ur — Change
ət^{h}yya — Alone
ətonlan — Float
ətoṛ — Win
ətoṛəyəy — Able
ətoṛəcay — End
ətoṛna — York
ətoṛtukomləy — Infinite
ətun — Now
ətuy — Liquid
ətuy — Soup
əyak — Shame
əyni — We
əyninu — Our
əyoŋ — fly (v)
əyoŋta — Fall
əyoṛ — Vend
əypa — June
əyṛo — Sale

əyru	Bone
ə-waṛ	Light
əwom	Black
əwonlien	Humble
əwoṛ	Throw
əwoy	Flesh
əwun	Skin
akicuun	Vibrate
alu	Potato
ar	Chicken
arkhoŋ	Cock
arne	Chicken
arpi	Hen
aṛsi	Star
artok	Duck
aṛtuy	Egg
ayt^{h}iyiŋ	Ginger
bak	Bat
ban	Get
ban	Arm
be	Bean
beheṛ	Clay
bel	jar
beləndri	Ladies finger
beyaŋ	Soyabean

b^hut	Devil
biet	Berry
bindu	Zero
birip	December
bol	Ball
$bopk^hət$	Pair
bor/p^hur	Basket
$boṛ/p^huṛ$	Some
bu	Cooked rice
bu	Rice
bubeŋ	Morsel
bulut	Starve
bulut	Famine
cəbuo	Tea-leaf
cəkma	Cucumber
cəcay	Rice
cəl	Forehead
cəmpra	Lemon
cəŋ	Right
cəy	Spear
ca	Tea
ca	Paddy
cainanəw	Brother's wife (y)
caypi	March
cak	Eat

caklenek	Food
caluŋləy	Mourn
caŋ	Trap
caŋ	Net
ce	Go
ce	Walk
ce	Paper
cek	Brick
cekpəl	Wall
cemte	Knife
cemyam	Dagger
cen	Zip
cənnəp^{h}a	Meal
cikməm	Spider
cil	Spit
ciŋ	Hill
ciŋcep	Wedge
cini	Sugar
citrat	Fear
cokcəl	Snail
cokk^{h}ʊy	Twist
cokki	Chair
col	Rest
con	Duty
coŋban	Word

coŋboy	Dumb
coŋciem	Fun
coŋcop	Taboo
coŋt^{h}əŋ	News
cop	Lungs
cuon	Work
cuonpek	Appoint
cur	Catch
cuṛ	Chase
curt^{h}a	Rainy season
curti	Noise
dəy	Like
dəy	Want
dəyt^{h}əŋ	Choice
day	Modest
del	Mud
dəŋk^{h}o	Lap
duktoŋ	Fail
eksen	Diarrhoea
el	thigh
en	Look
ersək	Jealous
eṛt^{h}a	October
g^{h}ari	Watch
gaw	Frog

həko/hənnako	And
həpta	Week
həpta/karkʰət	Week
həwahən	There
həycoy	Bring
ha	Teeth
haŋ/tʰep	Fold
haruy	gum
hay	Bake
henəye/hunəye	Where
heṛkʰət	Half
hin	Here
hiŋahi	So
hiwahi	It
hol	Sail
hoŋkeṛtʰokna	Origin
hoŋsoknəmun	Source
hoyyəyro	Wish
humpi/kamkəy	Tiger
in	Sleep
in	house
in	Drink
incuŋ	Roof
inkʰaṛ	Door
inkil	Kitchen

inkotte	Window
inṛik	Wall-lizard
insa	Cattle
inte	Cottage
ip^{h}up	Spring
it^{h}ət	Island
ituywan	Swim
jamp^{h}oŋ	Jack-fruit
jannin	Yesterday
jiŋpi	August
jiyiŋteŋ	Morning
joŋ	Monkey
jop	Kiss
kəyt^{h}iel	Market
kəl	Save
kəldak	Ladder
kəldakban	Step
kəpot^{h}əy	Pomegranate
kəy	I
kəykiyin	Garden lizard
kəynu	Me
kəysok	Invent
kəyta	My
ka	Room
kakru	Chalk

kaŋcotrol	Young
kaŋkəl	Mosquito-net
kaŋŋa	Goose
kaŋsi	Bell
kaŋtr˥um	Bowl
kant^{h}ə	Quilt
kap	Shoot
kari	Vehicle
kaykolen	Cradle
ke	Feet
kecun	Tremble
kedil	Heel
kehil	Round
kehu	Wheat
kek^{h}op	Shoe
kekiet	Lame
kel	Goat
keldoy	Sheep
kellet	Try
keməl	Toe(s)
keṛəŋ	Equal
keṛcat	Bug
keṛcu	Teach
keṛcu	learn
keṛdəŋ	Answer

Koireng	English
keṛday	Play
keṛdayna	Toy
keṛeŋpi	Oppose
kerhuoŋ	Riddle
keṛjoṛ	Weld
kerkay	Game
keṛk^{h}əlna	Consider
keṛminlen/əor	Proud
keṛmu	Meet
keṛŋəw	Quarrel
keṛŋay	Thought
keṛnok	Rock
keṛp^{h}ut	Decide
keṛret	Care
keṛrit^{h}okna	Dress
keṛrolla	Conspire
keṛsem	Divide
keṛsen	Divorce
keṛseso	Hurt
keṛt^{h}əŋ	Select
keṛt^{h}əy	Wait
keṛt^{h}eŋ	Collide
keṛt^{h}ol	Loose
keṛt^{h}y	Rise
keṛtocənp^{h}ut	Gentle

k^{h}ətk^{h}ətta	Each
k^{h}əwbuṛ	Common cold
k^{h}amul	Moustache
k^{h}aŋlay	Cockroach
k^{h}ar	Ban
k^{h}aṛ	Shut
k^{h}ason	Garlic
k^{h}ay	Grass-hopper
k^{h}ay	Frying pan
k^{h}aykolilok	Nightingale
k^{h}eŋ	Plate
k^{h}eŋ	Pot
k^{h}itk^{h}ay	Hang
k^{h}oboỹ	Late
k^{h}oi	Bee
k^{h}oi	Honey bee
k^{h}olsa	Lion
k^{h}omakkersam	Oath
k^{h}oŋkraw	Trouser
k^{h}oŋluŋni	Friday
khoŋup	Shoe
khoppi	Town
k^{h}opu	Witch
k^{h}unuk^{h}ərəŋ	Hawk
khuo	Village

k^{h}uṛ	Well
k^{h}urwadop	Well
k^{h}ylieŋ	Wax
kiby	Depend
kicəw	Bed sheet
kicoŋop	Jump
kine	Father's sister
$kink^{h}$ət	One
kinni	Two
kino	Date-palm
kinote	Aunt
kinthum	Three
$kint^{h}$umsunna	Third
kinu	Mother
kinulien	Mother's sister (e)
kinuməy	Wife
kinute	mother's sister(y)
kinute	Cousin (sister)
kipa	Daddy (father)
kipalien	Father's brother (e)
kipasien	Fathers brother (y)
kipate	Cousin (brother)
kipu	Mother's brother
kircorikəl	Shore
kiriet	Eight

kirietsunna	Eighth
kirki	Parrot
ki-təroy	Father-in-law
kitəɽpi	Mother-in-law
kit^{h}em	Sneeze
kitok	Seek
kitu	Spade
kiu	Elder
kiunu	Sister-in-law
kiunulien	Sister (e)
kiunute	Sister (y)
kiupa	Brother (e)
ko	Nine
kobi	Cabbage
kolkay	Sweet potato
kolom	Pen
kommila	Orange
koŋ	Waist
konuŋ	Palace
kopi	Cabbage
kopit^{h}əcet	Cauliflower
koɽ	Ear
koɽset	Deaf
kosunna	Ninth
kot	Coat

kultin	Nail
kum	Year
kum	Age
kumtʰəɽ	New year
kuruk	Six
kuruksunna	Sixth
kut	Hand
kutcəl	Index/Iron finger
kutki	ring
kutki	Elbow
kutlayta	Middle finger
kutməl	Ginger
kutninəy	Wrist
kutpʰa	Palm
kutpi	Thump
kuttenieŋ	Little finger
kuttin	Claw
ləyhaw	Soil
ləyŋoyɽəm	Desert
ləmpi	Road
ləttelməysər	Lantern
ləy	Tongue
ləyhariŋ	Fresh
ləykʰət	Repeat
ləyliay	Medicine

ləymay	Floor
ləypil	Earth
ləyroŋ	Demand
la	Song
lam	Dance
laŋkiya	Eagle
larik	Book
lat^{h}əw	Sing
lay	Naval
lemlet	Cheat
lien	Large
lien	Big
likli	Bottle
lilieŋ	Ornament
lilim	Picture
lilim	Shadow
lilin	Image
lillo	Joints
limol	Jute
liŋ	Thorn
$lisiŋk^{h}$ət	One thousand
lisiŋko	Nine thousand
lisiŋminli	Four thousand
lisiŋni	Two thousand
lisiŋriet	Eight thousand

lisiŋriŋŋa	Five thousand
lisiŋruk	Six thousand
lisiŋsəri	Seven thousand
lisiŋsom	Ten thousand
lisiŋtʰum	Three thousand
lon	Travel
lu	Head
luk	Enter
lum	Heat
luŋ	Stone
luŋ	Heart
luŋəl	Bold
luŋpʰur	Insects
luŋtʰək	Anger
lunut	Headache
lutʰ ok	Brain
məŋ	Harm
məŋkəl	Pea
məŋke	Tamarind
məy	Fire
məyhol	Coal
mərca	Pepper
məsək	Advance
mana	Prize
maṛtieŋ	South

mateŋ	Before
may	Pumpkin
may	Face
me	Meat
melma	Enemy
melsiet	Ugly
meŋsel	Looking glass
mertun	April
meru	Thief
mici	Salt
miciet	Ride
micituy	Saline
micu	Sugar cane
miju	Rat
mik^{h}oy	Break
milem	Vulture
miletmik^{h}up	Antonym
mince	Send
minci	Threat
miŋ	Name
minil	Forget
minkeɽcun	Annex
minkeɽcun	Unite
minkeɽcun	Combine
minkeɽcun	Compose

minli	Four
minlisunna	Fourth
minməŋhot	Destroy
minmu	Show
mint^{h}əyt^{h}eŋ	Define
miṛca	Chilli
miremmikənni	Saturday
misiel	Glass
mit	Eye
mitboṛ	Eye-lash
mitcəw	Blind
mitco	Blind
mit^{h}əy	Fly
mit^{h}em	Console
mit^{h}i	Tear
mitmul	eyebrow
moja	Shocks
moŋ/toṛ	Hip
monpak	Mattress
mot	banana
moyroy	Marriage
mrcariŋ	Green chilli
mu	See
muk	Ink
mukp^{h}u	Ink-pot

myri	Flame
nəktip	Day after tomorrow
nəmcənna	Quench
nəŋ	You
nəŋni	You (pl)
nəŋta	Your
nəynak	Thing
nəynakyoŋkoy	Decade
nəypillay	Surface
na	Ill
nai	Thatch
namək^{h}ətwat	Handicap
naŋ	Sliced bamboo
narṛ	Nose
naspati	Pear
nay	Child
naycənəy	Midwife
naypəŋ	Baby
naypəŋ	Children
nayte	Child
neṛ	Lip(s)
neṛ	Mouth
ŋəṛ	Hard
ŋəy	Sharp
ŋəyləy	Blunt

ŋa	Fish
ŋay	Hear
ŋaytoŋ/meŋte	Cat
ni	Sun
nik^{h}ətni	Day before yesterday
nikiṛ	Hate
niŋsət	Glad
niŋsiet	Love
niŋsiet	Dear
nipuytuk	Quite
niraŋniləl	Great
nisokteŋ	East
nitatteŋ	Evening
nom	Agree
nopkasik	Future
noy	World
nuk	Back
nukcum	Delay
nukka	After
nulcənday	Calm
num	Also
numəy	Woman
numəyte	Girl
nutkeṛen	Treatment
nutsietwoy	Disease

nuy	Laugh
nuy	smile
o	Yes
oŋ	Sit
oynu	Crane
pəl	Gate
pəncəwtʰur	Tomato
pənco	Brinjal
pəŋ	Fool
pət	Thread
pət	Thatch
pəttəm	Cotton
pəysa/dəŋka	Coin
pəysarat	Debt
pa	Read
paŋləy/əsuol	Coward
pasəl	Man
pasəlte	Boy
patʰien	God
pek	Give
pelep	Butterfly
pencil	pencil
per̥	Reap
pʰəlbipʰa	Winter
pʰəw	Shield

p^{h}əywo	Air
p^{h}eṛ	Mat
p^{h}ilt^{h}ət	Charm
p^{h}ukləy	Breathe
p^{h}uŋ	Surname
p^{h}urpa	May
p^{h}utna	Begin
p^{h}əyworaŋhiyəy	Breeze
pil	Page
pon	Cloth
ponsil	Quilt
ponsuymi	Tailor
puk^{h}ri	Tank
puk^{h}ri	Pond
puŋ	Hour
puŋəyton	Guava
puribə	Multiply
ṛəm	Country
rəm	Wild
ṛəm artok	Wild duck
rəmk^{h}əy	Zone
ṛəmsel	Wild cow
ṛəmsulkar	Den
ṛəmuy	Fox
ṛəmwok	Wild pig

rəp	Rush
ṛəp	Soon
ṛəy	Axe
ṛəykol	Garden
rəysuuop	Event
ra	Bear
ral	War
ṛalmi	Soldier
ralpəl	Fort
reŋ	King
ṛihu	Stream
rik	Heavy
ṛik^{h}o	Life
riki	Horn
rikoŋ	Ship
ṛikuwoŋ	Boat
ril	Inquire
ril	Say
ṛil	Speak
ṛilkel	Ask
rilkumpu	Prose
ṛilsuop	Express
rim	Smell
riŋŋa	Five
riŋŋasunna	Fifth

rinu	Breast
ṛisa	Voice
risa	Sound
risay	Collect
$rit^{h}a$	Soul
$rit^{h}aruy$	Nerve
ritun	Fever
riyak^{h}ət	One hundred
riyako	Nine hundred
riyaminli	Four hundred
riyani	Two hundred
riyariet	Eight hundred
riyariŋŋa	Five hundred
riyaruk	Six hundred
riyasəri	Seven hundred
riyat^{h}um	Three hundred
riyuŋ	Root
ro	Bamboo
ro	Rain
ṛoday	Dew
rolt^{h}əṛ/rot^{h}ər	Bachelor
ṛoŋru	Back-bone
ṛoṛi	Thunder
ru	Seed
rukt^{h}əw	Steal

ruməŋ	Dream
ruməy	Tail
ṛuolkeṛlop	Friend
ṛup^{h}el	Bow
ruy	Rope
səcak	Grass
səkhi	Deer
seləwwe	Buffalo
sələy	Evil
sələy	Wicket
səm	Hair
səmepmi	Barber
səŋ	Blur
səŋoŋsəy/səriŋsəy	Camel
sənna	Aid
səri	Seven
sərisunna	Seventh
sət	Beauty
səwəm	Bear
səy	Length
sa	Animal
sa/st	Good
sajokin henəmo/hunəmo	Zoo
saldum	Mole
samul	Wool

samulpon	Woolen cloths
samulpuon	Wool
saɪj	Tall
saŋsan	Mosquito
sapon	Soap
saypi	Elephant
seek	cow-dung
sek	farmer
sekel	Donkey
sek^{h}or	Horse
selatcəl	Bull
selay	Gun
sepəl	Wall
seratcəl	Bull
seratmesa	Beef
seratpi	Cow
serikul/sekuol	Cow-shed
serinutuy	Milk
serinutuyp^{h}ən	Cheese
serinutuytt^{h}ay	Butter
sete	Calf
simbu	Owl
sin	Small
sinsət	Derive
sinteŋ	North

so	Key
solien	Yale
som	Ten
somk^{h}ət	Eleven
somko	Ninety
somkoləyk^{h}ət	Ninety one
somkoləyko	Ninety nine
somkoləyli	Ninety four
somkoləyni	Ninety two
somkoləyriet	Ninety eight
somkoləyriŋŋa	Ninety five
somkoləyruk	Ninety six
somkoləysəri	Ninety seven
somkoləyt^{h}um	Ninety three
somləyko	Nineteen
somləyli	Fourteen
somləyni	Twelve
somləytiet	Eighteen
somləyriŋŋa	Fifteen
somləyruk	Sixteen
somləysəri	Seventeen
somləyt^{h}um	Thirteen
somminli	Forty
somminliləyk^{h}ət	Forty one
somminliləyko	Forty nine

somminliləyli	Forty four
somminliləyni	Forty two
somminliləyriet	Forty eight
somminliləyriŋŋa	Forty five
somminliləyruk	Forty six
somminliləysəri	Forty seven
somminliləyt^{h}um	Forty three
somni	Twenty
somniləyk^{h}ət	Twenty one
somniləyko	Twenty nine
somniləyli	Twenty four
somniləyni	Twenty two
somniləyriet	Twenty eight
somniləyriŋŋa	Twenty five
somt^{h}umləyruk	Thirty six
somniləysəri	Twenty seven
somniləyt^{h}um	Twenty three
somriet	Eighty
somrietləyk^{h}ət	Eighty one
somrietləyko	Eighty nine
somrietləyli	Eighty four
somrietləyni	Eighty two
somrietləyriet	Eighty eight
somrietləyriŋŋa	Eighty five
somrietləyruk	Eighty six

somrietləysəri	Eighty seven
somrietləyt^{h}um	Eighty three
somriŋŋa	Fifty
somriŋŋaləyk^{h}ət	Fifty one
somriŋŋaləyko	Fifty nine
somriŋŋaləyli	Fifty four
somriŋŋaləyni	Fifty two
somriŋŋaləyriet	Fifty eight
somriŋŋaləyriŋŋa	Fifty five
somriŋŋaləyruk	Fifty six
somriŋŋaləysəri	Fifty seven
somriŋŋaləyt^{h}um	Fifty three
somruk	Sixty
somrukləyk^{h}ət	Sixty one
somrukləyko	Sixty nine
somrukləyli	Sixty four
somrukləyni	Sixty two
somrukləyriet	Sixty eight
somrukləyriŋŋa	Sixty five
somrukləyruk	Sixty six
somrukləysəri	Sixty seven
somrukləyt^{h}um	Sixty three
somsəri	Seventy
somsəriləyk^{h}ət	Seventy one
somsəriləyko	Seventy nine

somsərilәyli	Seventy four
somsərilәyni	Seventy two
somsərilәyriet	Seventy eight
somsərilәyriŋŋa	Seventy five
somsərilәyruk	Seventy six
somsərilәysəri	Seventy seven
somsərilәyt^{h}um	Seventy three
somsunna	Tenth
somt^{h}um	Thirty
somt^{h}umlәyk^{h}ət	Thirty one
somt^{h}umlәyko	Thirty nine
somt^{h}umlәyli	Thirty four
somt^{h}umlәyni	Thirty two
somt^{h}umlәyriet	Thirty eight
somt^{h}umlәyriŋŋa	Thirty five
somt^{h}umlәyruk	Thirty six
somt^{h}umlәysəri	Thirty three
somt^{h}umlәyt^{h}um	Thirty three
sona	Gold
soŋkol	Shirt
soŋni	Sunday
suəncim	Mid-day
sump^{h}ay	Cloud
suoŋ	Cook
təkpə	Rub

təksa	Body
təl/waypol	Bread
tət	Sorrow
tan	Run
tankersiet	Race
taytak	West
taytakteŋ	West
tebəl	Table
teləŋga	Kite
telt^{h}uni	Tuesday
teŋwoŋ	Cage
tet	Keep
t^{h}əl	Arrow
t^{h}əmt^{h}uni	Wednesday
t^{h}əmuṛ	July
t^{h}əp^{h}əl	November
t^{h}əro	Lily
t^{h}ət	Kill
thəw	Calculate
t^{h}əwk^{h}ir	Again
t^{h}əy	Know
t^{h}əy	Fruit
t^{h}əybom	Grapes
t^{h}əyhay	Mango
t^{h}əyk^{h}a	Plum

t^{h}əyt^{h}up	Apple
t^{h}əytuy	Juice
t^{h}a	Month
t^{h}a	Moon
t^{h}an	Grave
t^{h}ap	Hide
t^{h}arəm	September
t^{h}aṛilni	Full-moon
t^{h}asiet	Idle
t^{h}at^{h}i	New-moon
t^{h}i	Blood
t^{h}iempu	Local physician
t^{h}inərəp	Danger
t^{h}iŋ	Wood
t^{h}iŋ	Tree
t^{h}iŋ	Fire-wood
t^{h}iŋcəkma	Papaya
t^{h}iŋcəŋ	Branch
t^{h}iŋkaŋ	Reed
t^{h}iŋkoṛ	Bark
t^{h}ir	Iron
t^{h}iraŋ	Wind
t^{h}iraŋ/p^{h}ywo	Air
t^{h}irhayho	Spoon
t^{h}iṛjop	Magnet

tʰoŋ	Bridge
tʰurumiŋ	Story
tiktiniŋ	Cuckoo
tilləw	Onion
tilpat	Leech
tiŋ	Cane
tok	Touch
toltaŋ	Court-yard
toŋləy	Busy
towulbuwol	January
toṛna	Last
tuy	Water
tuybol	Bath
tuyduŋ	River
tuylayluŋ	Ocean
tuytan	Current
tuytʰəmpi	Ocean
tuywaduŋ	River
u	a frog
ulənay	Brother
um	Tumbler
umtʰum	Gourd
upa	Old
upu	Almirah
upu	Box

uṛ	Snow
utp^{h}u	Dust
uy	Dog
uyrəyni	Thursday
uyte	Puppy
wəkir	Return
wa	Bird
wa	Come
wacek	Sparrow
waak	Crow
wakkəykoŋ	King fisher
wakuwoŋ	Peacock
walolna	Journey
wan	Sky
waneṛ	Beak
waŋwoy	Fog
wanoyləysiet	Earth
waribu	Nest
wasu	Pigeon
wat	Reduce
watuŋ	Arrive
wayk^{h}u	Lock
wen	Today
wienin	Today
wok	Beat

wok	Pig
wokkicon	Hit
wokme	Pork
won	Belly
woncam	Appetite
wonpor	Indigestion
wont^{h}eŋ	Honest
woy	left
wulpi	February
wuṛ	Ice
wuṛkay	Bouquet
wut	Ash
wuysteŋdot	Dragonfly
yək	Insult
yək	Tame
yəyni	Monday
yaəncim	Mid-night
yaksəṛ	Bracelet
yalk^{h}um	Bad
yalk^{h}um	Bed
yamyəl	Tire
yan	Night
yantieŋ	Yesterday
yikeŋ	Morning
yi-tieŋ	Tomorrow

yomsət	Ideal
yu	Liquor
yulewa	Animal
yupi	Coconut

Bibliography

Chhangte, Lalnunthangi, 1986, *A Preliminary Grammar of Mizo Language* (Unpublished M.A. Dissertation) University of Texas.

_______, 1986, *The Grammar of Simple Clauses in Mixo*. In David Bradly (ed) South East Asian Linguistics, 95-174, Pacific Linguistics

Cornyn, W.S. and H.D. Roof, 1968, *Beginning of Burmese*. Yale University Press.

Jones, Robert B. Jr. 1961, *Karen Linguistics Studies*, University of California Press.

Koshal, Sanyukta, 1979, *Ladakhi Grammar*, Motilal Banarasidas, Delhi

Park, Jang Sik, 1995, *Burmese Phonology and Morphology* (unpublished Ph.D Thesis) Banaras Hindu University, Varansi.

Sharma, D.D. 1988. *A Descriptive Grammar of Kinnauri*. Mittal Publications, Delhi

Shigh, Chungkham Yashawanta, 2000, *Manipuri Grammar*, Rajesh Publication, New Delhi

________, 2002, *Tarao Grammar*, Akansha Publishing House, New Delhi

Thurgood, Graham and Randy J. Lapolla (edited) 2003. *The Sino-Tibetan Languages.*

Trudgill, p.1986, Scociolinguistics; *An Introduction to Language and Society, Harmondsworth: Penguin Books.*